Organized Teacher, Happy Classroom

A Lesson Plan for Managing Your Time, Space and Materials

Melanie S. Unger

BETTERWAY HOME
CINCINNATI, OHIO
WWW.BETTERWAYBOOKS.COM

Other fine Betterway Home Books are available from your local bookstore and
online suppliers. Visit our website, www.betterwaybooks.com.

15 14 13 12 11   5 4 3 2 1

ISBN-13: 978-1-4403-0915-1

Distributed in Canada by Fraser Direct
100 Armstrong Avenue, Georgetown, Ontario, Canada L7G 5S4, Tel: (905) 877-
4411

Distributed in the U.K. and Europe by F&W Media International, LTD
Brunel House, Forde Close, Newton Abbot, TQ12 4PU, UK, Tel: (+44) 1626
323200, Fax: (+44) 1626 323319, E-mail: enquiries@fwmedia.com

Distributed in Australia by Capricorn Link
P.O. Box 704, S. Windsor NSW, 2756 Australia, Tel: (02) 4577-3555

Edited by Jacqueline Musser
Designed by Clare Finney
Production coordinated by Mark Griffin

Melanie Unger has been a classroom teacher for more than seventeen years and strives daily to instill organizing principles within her personal and professional life and in her students' lives. She started a professional organizing business in 2008, following her dream of supporting others in discovering meaningful and sustainable organizing solutions in order to become more productive and lead happier, more inspired lives. Melanie has both a bachelor's and a master's degree in Education. She is a member of the National Association of Professional Organizers (NAPO) and Faithful Organizers. She teaches fifth grade in Dublin, Ohio. She and her husband enjoy playing with (and spoiling) their adorable black lab, Shelby.

Visit her website: www.organizedinspirations.com.

Dedication

To my grandparents, Floyd and Opal, who inspired me to always appreciate life, to walk wisely, and to surround myself with the qualities of hard work, education, dedication, love, and humility. Their example of love, care, and devotion is one I try to emulate on a daily basis. They are present in my life in so many ways each day.

To my Dad, who I miss each day, but treasure in my heart always.

Acknowledgments

Writing a book has been a dream of mine for more than twenty years. Many people have been major players in helping this dream come to fruition.

I first and foremost want to thank my husband, Doyle, who stood by me through the process, always encouraging me and exhibiting such patience while I spent many, many hours writing this book. He is a wonderful supporter and an amazing, caring husband! I'm truly blessed to have him in my life.

Thanks to my mother, Marilyn, who is a remarkable, positive role model in so many ways. She dares to dream with me in whatever I choose to do, all the while sharing her thoughts, suggestions, and unwavering support and wisdom along the way. She is truly the "wind beneath my wings."

I want to thank my sisters, Amy and Megan, for their unwavering support and love. I am richly blessed because of their presence in my life, and I'm so proud to call them my sisters. Thanks also to their husbands, Dennis and Denny, and to my beautiful niece, Audrey.

Thanks to my extended family, as well as my in-laws, David, Euniece, Darlene, Larry, Janell, and Amanda, for all of your support and love.

I would be remiss if I didn't thank my principal and colleagues at school for their support. I am so thankful to work with such hard-working, caring professionals. Thanks to my fifth-grade team and hallway buddies for being enthusiastic supporters. A special thanks to Sharon, Cindy S., and Judi for their organizing ideas, contributions, and encouragement.

Thanks to all of the wonderful friends in my life. Thanks to Derek for providing a positive word just when I needed to finish a chapter or push forward to meet a deadline. You are a dear friend. Thanks to Gloria for her encouragement and friendship. Thanks to Bruce for his listening ear and encouragement about this book project. Stevo and Chika, your positive words mean so much. Thanks for encouraging me in this journey.

Thanks to all of the students I've had the pleasure of teaching in the past seventeen-plus years (and thanks to their parents, too). Their enthusiasm for learning and growing makes teaching worthwhile. They've helped me learn so much, especially about how to become a more organized teacher!

Thank you to Jackie, my editor at Betterway Home Books, who from the start supported me and helped answer any questions I had along the way. Thanks for your thoughtful editing suggestions and for choosing me to represent this book concept.

Thanks to Jim Moats and Jackie Hagar for their advice and professionalism. I truly enjoyed working with you during this book project.

Finally, I thank God for providing me the ability to write, and for the desire to share a little of myself through two of my great passions—organizing and teaching—through this book. It is through faith in Him that I could complete this project.

Contents

Introduction

"Good order is the
foundation of all things."
— Edmund Burke

Based on my more than seventeen years as an educator, and now also as a professional organizer, I believe that most teachers are inherently organized, at least on a basic level. The very nature of our job forces us to multitask on a variety of levels, from lesson planning to preparing student materials. If we didn't incorporate basic organizing principles into our days, we wouldn't get very far as professionals. But we all know our good intentions and even strong beginnings can quickly fade as the pace of the school year quickens. With the multitude of tasks and responsibilities teachers face daily, organizing our classrooms can easily become a secondary priority.

But I believe an organized room must be at the forefront of our plans for successful school years. Without organized classrooms, we cannot ensure that our lessons are sound, our materials are accounted for, or our classroom spaces are functional and useful for our students.

> Without an organized classroom, we cannot ensure that our lessons are sound, our materials are accounted for, or our classroom spaces are functional and useful for our students.

Whether you teach primary, intermediate, middle school, or high school students, this book is meant to be a guide that helps you realize your goals for becoming more organized with your time, paperwork, and classroom spaces. There is really no right or wrong way to be organized. Teachers must decide for themselves what being organized means.

It's also important to remember that there is no magic level of organization (we never really arrive at the pinnacle of organization). Being organized requires regular maintenance. What is important is to find a level of organization that will

- help you promote a calm, caring environment
- support you in carrying out effective instruction
- allow you to find, use, and manage materials, supplies, and resources easily and efficiently

Each chapter in this book addresses a main focus area of organizing. You might choose to read it through from cover to cover, or you can turn directly to a specific section of the book that will help you with a problem area.

At the conclusion of each chapter, you'll find a checklist that highlights the key themes, ideas, and action items from the chapter. Use these lists as springboards to help you organize your own classroom. In the appendix, you'll find templates for forms and charts that you can photocopy and use in your own classroom and in your teacher reference binder.

This book is not a how-to book in the traditional sense. I won't be telling you exactly how you should organize your desk or storage cabinets. I won't be sharing the one best way to organize your files or your classroom library. Throughout this book, however, I'll share several strategies to enrich your existing organizational skills. I will highlight areas of organization that I consider to be critical for an educator and provide strategies for these areas so you can be truly prepared for your busy days with students. I've used these principles and organizing ideas in my own classroom, and I've helped other teachers implement them through my role as a professional organizer. I write from the perspective of a fellow educator and include advice and tips from my background as a professional organizer.

What is important is to find a level of organization that will help you promote a calm, caring environment; support you in carrying out effective instruction; and allow you to find, use, and manage materials, supplies, and resources easily and efficiently.

Since I started teaching, I've come to understand that a teacher's level of organization (or lack thereof) has a direct impact on students' learning and motivation. Additionally, I've found that my own level of organization in my teaching career has largely affected my overall peace of mind. I've found that being highly organized is a true asset to the teaching profession, one about which I am deeply passionate.

> A teacher's level of organization (or lack thereof) has a direct impact on students' learning and motivation.

Most of all, I wrote this book because I believe that organizing is indeed a good thing, a positive and achievable goal, and in most respects, a fun process. I look forward to helping you become an organized teacher and create a happy classroom!

1: The Benefits of an Organized Classroom

"Simplicity is the ultimate sophistication."

— Leonardo da Vinci

One of the most important reading strategies I teach my students each year is that of visualizing. I ask my students to really picture in their minds what is happening in the story to help them better connect and relate to the events and characters within the book. Visualizing also helps students solidify and deepen their comprehension because they are actively constructing meaning. So let's use this strategy when thinking about organizing your classroom. Picture in your mind what you really want when you think of an organized classroom.

The answer may seem obvious at first. You may be thinking, "Organized is organized, right?" Well, in a way, this is true, but generalities aside, we need to remember that the definition of what it means to be an organized teacher differs quite a bit from person to person. Be specific and concrete about what you perceive would contribute to your most organized classroom space.

Sometimes it may be easy to picture another teacher's classroom and think, "Oh, I would love to have a classroom like that!" This is a fine approach if you have specific reasons for organizing your room that way and you plan to put many of that teacher's organizing systems in place within your own classroom. But also be realistic so you are reasonable about your organizing expectations. Consider your own personality, style, and personal preferences. What works for one teacher may not work for another. No organizing style is superior to another. If your organizing style works for you, it is a successful style.

What ideas or words come to mind when you visualize an organized classroom? Do you think of *calm* and *peaceful*, or perhaps even *controlled*? Maybe the words *serene* or *relaxed* cross your mind. What about *functional*, *clean*, or maybe *warm* and *inviting*? Think about which of these descriptors (or aspects of these descriptors) play a part in your vision for an organized classroom. Although it is true that it can be difficult to maintain a sense of order and organization in a classroom (especially throughout the school year), there are

In the midst of all of the pressures we face as teachers, we may not consider how staying organized can help us on a daily basis.

specific, positive benefits to setting up appropriate and realistic systems for organizing your classroom spaces. In the midst of all of the pressures we face as teachers, we may not consider how staying organized can help us on a daily basis.

Let's look at some of the benefits of an organized classroom. There are sure to be many more, but here are some of the most meaningful ones. Which of these benefits is most important to you?

GAIN PEACE OF MIND

Let's face it, an organized classroom has a calming effect. Even if everything else around us seems chaotic, when we have a sense of organization in our classrooms, we feel like we can put one foot in front of the other and make the most of our day. When we are organized, we know where to find the next day's worksheets, the following day's math quiz, and this Friday's science materials. We can breathe deeply (if only for a short time) and appreciate our sense of organization. Organizational structures must be in place to develop peace of mind in an otherwise busy, stressful day in the life of a teacher.

ACHIEVE A SENSE OF CONTROL

Oftentimes as teachers we don't feel in control of our days. Although much of the school day includes routines that are familiar, and though we plan accordingly, a variety of interruptions can sometimes leave us feeling like we are failing to make progress. This can be especially difficult for teachers with "Type A" personalities (which many teachers, myself included, possess) who like to know what is coming around each and every corner. The reality for us is that we often must "roll with the punches," so to speak. Being as organized as possible helps us gain some sense of control over our daily schedules.

When we gain some organizational control in our classrooms, we are free to focus on the most important things, including student performance and our curriculum.

INCREASE ENERGY LEVELS

We all know that the teaching profession, while hugely rewarding, is also stressful and taxing. Most of us are simply exhausted at the end of a busy day of teaching. Teaching requires a great deal of energy, concentration, focus, and creativity. Do you often feel, as I do, that you don't know how much more energy you could give after a day in the classroom? To become more efficient in our profession, we need to balance our lives in regard to our energy levels and how we recharge our batteries. I'll address this in more depth in Chapter 15, but it's important to acknowledge here as well. When we make a concerted organizing effort within our classrooms, I believe that we are, in effect, promoting a greater sense of energy for ourselves. Instead of using our energy to find lost papers, misplaced or improperly stored materials, or documents within our ineffective filing systems, we will have the energy we need to contribute toward planning effective instruction. We can engage our students in thoughtful discussions and assess student learning more efficiently. Being organized allows us to actually give more of ourselves—more of our energy—to the things that count!

> Organizational structures must be in place to develop peace of mind in an otherwise busy, stressful day in the life of a teacher.

SAVE TIME

As teachers, we wish we had more time. We need more time to plan lessons, grade papers, assess for individual needs, file papers, clean shelves or desks, organize our computer files…the list goes on and on. In fact, lacking time to do all of the things we need to do is probably one of the greatest concerns we face as teachers in the twenty-first century. We are hard-pressed to do more, plan more efficiently in order to remain accountable, assess more rigorously, and differentiate more meaningfully while still doing the tasks we have done in the past. These realities make the time you save one of the greatest benefits of keeping an organized classroom. When you are organized within your classroom, you will save time.

When you are more organized, you are capable of doing your work, which is teaching students, rather than looking for a worksheet, a piece of mail, or a student file. As with the benefit of increasing your energy level, you will have more of yourself to offer to students when you're organized.

REDUCE DISTRACTIONS

When we are overwhelmed in our classrooms, we tend to focus on the things that are in front of us—the messy piles, the shelves in disarray, or the disordered file cabinet. You might feel blocked from being totally effective in your work because these things are consistently hanging over your head. We need to find a way to manage this clutter. You may already have the resources and know-how needed

Get Organized, Gain Time

According to a 2008 National Association of Professional Organizers (NAPO) nationwide survey of four hundred consumers, 27 percent said they feel disorganized at work, and of those, 91 percent said they would be more effective and efficient if their work spaces were better organized. Twenty-eight percent said they would save more than an hour per day, and 27 percent said they would save thirty-one to sixty minutes each day.

to contain the clutter, but circumstances like time constraints or interruptions in your daily schedule may cause you to fail to keep these systems consistently well maintained. After you gain control over clutter and discover and maintain a set of organized systems for your classroom, you can resist or rid yourself of these distractions and get on with the important work of your day.

PROMOTE PRODUCTIVITY

We all know how wonderful it feels to go through the course of a day when we are on top of the world. You know what I mean, one of those days where you have everything planned thoroughly—your lesson plans are detailed, your worksheets are in order, your materials are ready—and you feel positive and energetic about the day ahead. This situation is sometimes the exception rather than the rule for many of us, in that our proverbial ducks are not always in a row. Sure, we may have several aspects of our day planned, but there always seems to be one or two areas that we wish we had structured more efficiently or planned differently. Incorporating several specific strategies for organizing your classroom will go a long way in helping you to become more productive over the course of a school year.

ACHIEVE CLARITY

When you have a solid sense of organization within your classroom, you'll achieve greater clarity in identifying educational goals for your students. Organizing allows you to put more energy into your curriculum standards. You can plan lessons more efficiently and, therefore, become more focused on clearly communicating objectives to students on a daily basis.

You will also be able to think more meaningfully about individual students' needs. Being a good teacher involves working hard to differentiate instruction for our students, guiding them in their learning based on their needs. When you are organized in your classroom, you will be able to home in on your students' needs with greater clarity because you are not distracted by clutter.

MEET CAREER GOALS

We all have different professional goals. Some teachers desire to work in one grade level for a long period of time. Others might specialize in a certain area of the curriculum, such as a specific subject. Others may want to eventually walk the path of an administrative role. Still others want to become well-rounded in all subject areas, fulfilling a role in a self-contained classroom. Professional goals are wide and varied, but becoming organized is one of the key factors toward meeting any goal, especially a professional goal. Chapter 14 has more on setting professional goals.

IMPROVE STUDENT PERFORMANCE

Perhaps one of the greatest benefits to becoming more organized in our classrooms is that, in so doing, we can focus on increasing student performance. We want to guide students toward becoming critical thinkers, reflective readers, and cooperative, helpful, inquisitive learners so we can support them in achieving the highest levels of performance. We desire, above nearly all else, to shape and mold our students, and part of that requires a well-functioning, safe environment where learning can take place. When we are truly organized teachers, it will reflect in our teaching practices. Organizing creates a domino effect. Start by organizing your classroom. That effort allows you to focus more effectively and efficiently deliver curricular lessons. In turn, students are more likely to pay attention to your objectives and perform more positively under your guidance and support.

Imagine a time in your teaching career when you felt unorganized. Now compare that experience to your most organized teaching moment. (If you are a new teacher, reflect on how your life was affected during a time when you were not as organized as you needed to be.) What things were different in this unorganized state? How did you approach the lesson or situation? Were you calm and confident or somewhat harried and stressed? How would you gauge your energy level? Were you engaged and enthusiastic or somewhat drained? Did you engage students in meaningful conversation, or was it somewhat forced because your plan was unclear? All of these things are part of carrying out an effective lesson. A solid sense of organization in our paperwork, our planning, our materials, and our classroom will help us in our efforts toward improved student motivation and performance.

> A solid sense of organization in our paperwork, our planning, our materials, and our classroom will help us in our efforts toward improved student motivation and performance.

TRANSFER OF SKILLS

In becoming more organized as a teacher and sharing various operational procedures or expectations with students, we are, in effect, transferring these organizational skills to our students. When we take the time to instruct students on how to organize their papers, materials, and storage areas (such as their desks or locker areas), we are setting students up for success from the first day of school. This is one of the most important benefits to having an organized classroom. To this end, I carve out structured time in my daily routine to emphasize to students some aspect of the importance of being organized. I tell them how being more organized can help them achieve a successful school year. I work with students, especially at the beginning of the year, but also throughout the school year as situations arise, to introduce and reinforce sound principles by which they can stay organized, so they begin to internalize these methods for themselves and determine other strategies for their future success in life. Chapters 12 and 13 feature several ways to help students become organized and stay organized throughout the year.

EXPERIENCE THE BENEFITS

Can having an organized classroom really produce all of the benefits described in this chapter? Yes, it can! Being an organized classroom teacher is not the answer to everything, but it will certainly go a long way in helping you achieve the goals you set for yourself as an educator. Being organized also helps propel you forward on your path toward becoming a more effective teacher. Having organizational systems in place gives you the ability to prepare for a successful school year. As you incorporate these changes into your classroom structure, you will notice a difference, and your students will, too.

The Benefits of an Organized Classroom

- [ ] Gain peace of mind
- [ ] Achieve a sense of control
- [ ] Increase energy levels
- [ ] Save time
- [ ] Reduce distractions
- [ ] Promote productivity
- [ ] Achieve clarity
- [ ] Meet career goals
- [ ] Improve student performance
- [ ] Transfer of skills

2: First Steps to an Organized Classroom

"Organizing is what you do
before you do something,
so that when you do it, it
is not all mixed up."

— A.A. Milne

When I hear a person quip about how much free time teachers have over summer break, I wonder if the person knows the extent of teachers' efforts and dedication levels. Many of our summers are spent revising units, preparing lessons, taking (or teaching) classes or working other jobs or businesses, while also trying to lead some semblance of a personal life. But, a little time away from the classroom can give you some perspective on how you've organized your classroom. You also can think about initiating some needed transformations in your room for the upcoming school year. One of the key steps to becoming (and staying) organized throughout the school year begins during the summer when you enter your room during those first few trips back. Reflecting on how your classroom is working (as well as how it's not working) helps you reframe the situation and think about how you can make positive changes in your classroom in the year ahead.

A TOUR OF YOUR ROOM

When you walk into your classroom those first few times in late summer, you no doubt begin to visualize and plan for the multitude of tasks that lie ahead. You may make detailed to-do lists, and begin thinking about planning curricular lessons and units. You need to determine the changes needed to organize your classroom, curriculum, and lessons. You need to identify these changes, and then make a plan for the upcoming school year. I suggest that we start with a thorough "tour" of your room.

Personally, the idea of taking a methodical, focused tour of my room is not natural for me. I tend to want to dig right in with a fury, and attack my supplies, materials, and any furniture that I can move around and get right back into place. Getting some immediate sense of order is important to me. Whether it is simply to move the student desks into an arrangement, move my teacher's desk back in the right spot, or put my filing cabinet in place, it just feels good to have some tangible things completed on that first day back in the classroom. I am a bit crazed the first couple of times I am back in my room because my goal, initially, is to achieve some sense of visual order again. But in recent years I have learned that I have greater success (and pave the way to a much calmer start to the school year) when I slow down and resist this urge to jump right in. When I think carefully about my classroom and realize the opportunity I have each fall to determine how to arrange my room and how to make changes that promote the best atmosphere for learning, I am so much the happier. I think you will be, too.

The Process

So, what does this tour involve? First, let me suggest that a room tour can be done any time of the school year. Sometimes it's easiest to address aspects of room organization in the summer just before the beginning of the school year when your stress level may be a bit lower. However, you can take steps toward organizing your classroom at any point in the year. Organizing is truly an ongoing process! This section explains a room tour in the time frame of late summer, just before school starts. Regardless of when you tour your classroom, the first step is taking time to study how your room looks in its current state.

If you are like me, seeing all of the materials, furniture, and supplies in disarray can be a bit uncomfortable. When we leave our classrooms at the end of the school year, we are usually asked to perform certain tasks dealing with organizing or storing our classroom furniture, materials, and supplies to allow the custodial staff to perform needed cleaning, repairs, or painting. In my own room, my student desks are usually uprooted (perhaps a bit haphazardly, off to one side of the room), and chairs are stacked several high away from the center of the room.

As you examine the room, record your thoughts so you can refer back to them. Jot down your thoughts about your desks. Are they at different heights? Has this been bothering you for years? Write any desired changes down on paper. Have you been thinking about moving the desks into a different configuration at the start of the year due to new research you've read? Jot that thought down. Do you need to consider adding some shelving or other storage pieces to your room?

Reflecting on these thoughts is an important step toward making positive changes in organizing your classroom. Skipping this step can keep you from making real changes that will help you become more organized. I am not saying that you need to make grand, sweeping changes—especially if you have systems that have worked well for you and your students. But if you are thinking that some changes are needed regarding the room's organization and arrangement, this step will be highly beneficial in making more of your organizing goals become a reality. For more ideas and prompting questions, see the Tour of Your Room Planning Sheet on page 205 in the appendix.

UNIQUE PREFERENCES AND TASTES

Each teacher has different aesthetic preferences and tastes for how to set up and maintain a classroom. He or she also has instructional differences and preferences. I have yet to see two classrooms that look or function exactly alike. There are so many considerations when thinking about a classroom and how to set it up. The important thing to remember is to think first about what *you* like and what style *you* have in mind for your room. Whether you are conscious of it or not, your classroom reflects who you are. From your desk arrangements to your classroom library setup (depending on your grade level or subject area) to your filing system to items such as rugs, lighting, and other accents, your room arrangement must make sense to you in both style and functionality. There is no one right way to do things. Instead, in this book, I aim to provide suggestions and tips that will guide you to think critically and make the best decisions for yourself so you can continue thinking about

> Your classroom reflects who you are.

the most important thing—your instruction! Throughout my years of teaching, I have worked hard to find systems that work for me on a consistent basis; these individual techniques seem to provide me with the most success from day to day. Having those organizing systems run like a well-oiled machine brings a sense of peace and calm to my day, even when a hundred other things are going on around me. Sound familiar?

STUDENT DESK ARRANGEMENTS

Teachers know the importance of properly arranging student desks. It's important to give student desk arrangements a lot of thought. Deciding upon and understanding the format of your students' desk placement from the first day forward can make a world of difference as you begin instruction with your students.

Desks in Pods

Teachers at various grade levels appreciate setting up desks in a pod format, with four to six desks in a group, to promote aspects of cooperative learning and a sense of community within the classroom. This configuration also typically promotes good traffic flow through the room because the grouping allows for more space between the pods.

Rounded Rows

Some teachers prefer an arrangement similar to traditional rows, but with a twist. The rounded row configuration preserves the idea of a row format, but instead of rigid, straight rows, the rows curve in a bit (almost in a rainbow shape), promoting a bit more conversation among students.

Modified Row Arrangement

Another possibility is a more modified row format, a sort of scattered arrangement. In this type of format, most desks are in row format, but with branches of desks coming off of the rows. Some teachers prefer this arrangement because it allows for students to face the front of the room, but still talk in groups of two or three.

U-Shaped Arrangement

A U-shaped arrangement allows for much more open discussion among students. This setup encourages the entire group to be part of class lessons, debates, or collaboration. Depending on the subject area, many middle and high school teachers appreciate this format because it promotes conversations and discussions appropriate for a variety of lessons within a given curriculum.

Change It Up

Whichever format you choose at the beginning of the year, I suggest that you consider shaking things up a bit and changing your desk format a couple of times during the year. A few years ago, when I had a particularly talkative class, I found that the six-person pod arrangement was just not working. The students were more naturally inclined to talk with their classmates during the day and were not paying as much attention during lessons. After I changed the desk arrangement to more of a modified row placement, I observed that students were more focused, and were participating more frequently, mostly due to this change. The bottom line, when it comes to desk arrangements, is to find an organizational setup that you like and to use the method that promotes the type of student behaviors you desire. It may take a few tries to figure it out, even for seasoned teachers, because each class is unique year to year and you'll need to find the arrangement that works for your current group of students.

Desks in pods

Desks in rounded rows

Desks in modified rows

Desks in U-shape

OTHER FURNITURE CONSIDERATIONS

We work in our classrooms for the better part of eight hours a day
(or more!), so we should carefully plan what other items to include
in our rooms to help promote efficiency as well as a warm, inviting
feel. I don't advocate going overboard, however, because you do have
specific considerations, including your district codes and health reg-
ulations to keep in mind. However, you might decide to bring some
simple items into your classroom so you can help students feel more
at home, more motivated, and generally calm and relaxed while they
are in your classroom. Think about what items you want to incorporate. Are you permitted to bring pillows, beanbags, or comfy chairs
or couches into your room? Does your room have space for these?
Carefully measure for these items, and be selective. Too many extra
items will turn into clutter. Look for furniture pieces that serve more
than one purpose whenever possible so you can bring fewer items
into your classroom, thereby cutting back on potential clutter. It's
really up to you to decide this for yourself. Sometimes the answer
comes from trying out different things and letting your preferences
come to the surface as you spend time in your classroom each day.
Here are some specific considerations for accessories:

Pillows and bean bags: These are great in reading nooks. How
many pillows do you need? How will you store the pillows—in a
basket or on the floor?

Lamps: Identify where you need additional lighting. It could be
a floor lamp in the reading nook or a desk lamp for your teacher's
desk.

Chairs, couches, or loveseats: This addition can help students feel
more comfortable reading and promote a warm and inviting atmosphere in the room. Choose something comfortable yet durable and
appropriately sized for your room and purpose.

In my classroom, I like having a barstool or some other type
of chair in which I can sit to address the class during announcements or during my structured read-aloud time. This stool or chair

can also serve other purposes, such as a reader's chair for sharing a book or students' writing pieces.

Wall art: In addition to student work and learning charts, sometimes it is a good idea to include beautiful artwork, paintings, or even framed quotes or sports team posters within the classroom. This gives your room personality.

Upper-level teachers sometimes create a colorful "graffiti" wall in the classroom for students to share compliments or positive experiences.

Plants: Real or artificial greenery makes the space feel a bit homier. They bring life and color to the room and can contribute to a sense of calm.

Area rugs: These are helpful in establishing zones or areas within a room, even if the room is carpeted. Rugs can add a splash of color as well as give the room a calm, relaxing touch. I use an area rug in my reading nook.

Taking the time to be thoughtful about furniture or accessories to include in your room allows you to be creative and put meaningful touches within your classroom spaces. Both you and your students will enjoy the time and effort you put into making these decisions because these items can help to promote a warm, inviting, calm feel in the room.

Use the Furniture Considerations Planning Sheet on page 206 in the appendix as you tour your room and think about additions to your classroom for the year.

The Importance of Shelving

Depending on what furniture was housed in your classroom before it became yours, there may be many shelves (built-in or stand-alone types) or perhaps (goodness forbid!) few or no shelves for storage. Even though it can be somewhat of an investment, I highly recommend that you purchase at least one or two shelving units. The reality is that you must create storage opportunities or you will not be able to properly contain or maintain all of the supplies and materials you need. Even the most organized of teachers cannot effectively manage materials without adequate shelving.

No matter which grade level you teach—elementary, middle, or high school—you need shelving space. If you lack shelves, ask your custodial staff if any extra shelving units exist in your building or within your school district. It never hurts to ask, and you might be surprised one day when you walk into your classroom and find a sturdy shelving unit there waiting for you to fill it!

PURGING

Although I've devoted a full chapter (Chapter 3) to the importance of and procedures for purging, I couldn't end this chapter without some initial thoughts on this all-important step toward an organized classroom.

First of all, many teachers have a love-hate relationship with throwing things away. The logic for many of us is to save everything because, as many teachers say, "I may need it someday." We are in a unique position sometimes to *not* throw things away, due to the sheer variety of materials and supplies needed to create engaging, interesting, and well-rounded lessons. So, keeping some things is important in order to have a supply of items on hand for various creative activities and lessons—beads, glitter, pipe cleaners, thread, and many other materials come to mind (especially for elementary teachers). You never know when you will need something, right? Well, sort of. I contend that having such supplies on hand is fine as long as you have proper systems for dealing with these items and as long as these items do not become a source of clutter.

Evaluate the items that you have, and determine what to keep. Purging starts with the act of taking an inventory of things and determining the value of each item, both for yourself and for your students. Be brutally honest, and it really will pay off in the end. Purging is not, as some think, a dirty word (although the act of purging itself can get rather messy). Commit to taking a moderate amount of time before the start of the school year to do some purging. It will be incredibly helpful toward creating a well-ordered classroom (the process can be superbly cathartic as well).

Congratulations on taking the first step toward making your classroom more organized, and good luck with your room tour. You may be tempted to skip this process so you can get straight to your to-do list (I can relate; that's my style), but I hope you see the value in taking time to evaluate and judge your room's needs. When you purposefully set out to think through this process and make some thoughtful changes to room arrangement and structure, you likely will need to make far fewer organizing adjustments in your room in the months ahead!

First Steps to an Organized Classroom

- ☐ Take a tour of your classroom and give serious thought to its layout. Use the Tour of Your Room Planning Sheet on page 205 for guidance.

- ☐ Identify your aesthetic and instructional preferences and tastes for your classroom layout.

- ☐ Select the arrangement of your students' desks.

- ☐ Identify extra items you want to bring into your classroom. Use the Furniture Considerations Planning Sheet on page 206 for guidance.

- ☐ Assess your shelf space and make arrangements to increase it if you need more.

3: The Power of Purging

"A journey of a
thousand miles begins
with a single step."
— Lao-tzu

I love the Lao-tzu quote at the beginning of this chapter because getting organized sometimes seems like a long journey. At times, we cannot see our destination because of the distance we need to travel. There is so much to consider in our classrooms, not only in the summer months when we are preparing for a new school year, but also throughout the year as we attempt to maintain systems while carrying out effective, engaging lessons for our students. One of the keys to maintaining organizing systems is purging.

What is purging? There are various dictionary definitions, but purging basically involves taking specific steps to eliminate clutter from our spaces in order to promote order and a sense of organization. Purging is about evaluating what you own and making smart decisions about the value of your possessions in regard to the space that you have. In order to set a proper mind-set for the process, it's important to really understand what purging involves. This understanding will make your purging more efficient. This chapter will explain in detail the steps to successful purging and give you a framework for how to effectively incorporate the habit of purging into your organizing systems to achieve your goals.

> Purging is about evaluating what you own and making smart decisions about the value of your possessions in regard to the space that you have.

THE BENEFITS OF PURGING

Sometimes when people hear the word "purge," they physically cringe. I can see their bodies tighten. Sometimes it can be an uncomfortable process, no doubt, but purging your spaces of items you no longer need or use can go a long way in helping you become more organized. Purging is a key step toward reaching long-term goals for organization, and it gives you a feeling of being more in control of your spaces because it helps you become more aware of what you have. It also helps you feel confident and proud of what you own. Purging can actually help you put more value on the things you own because, in keeping an item, you are saying that it is worthy of your attention. So purging is not just about throwing things away; it's about thinking critically about what you do own and putting pride into those items. Therefore, through the process of purging, a person can feel happier—somewhat lighter—both figuratively and literally! It's important to understand, too, that tackling the act of purging in your classroom should not be a once-in-a-lifetime experience (i.e., when you retire!), but should become part of a structured yearly routine to help you establish clutter-free spaces where you can do your best work in teaching your students.

ASSESSING NEEDS

When it comes to purging, the first thing you need to do is assess what actually needs to be in each space or area of the classroom. Often, this is not typically what a person thinks of first when he or she begins the purging process. Initially you might go to an area of your classroom and instantly tear into the space, not really thinking through how the space needs to function for you and whether you need to change aspects of the space to help you meet your goals.

With purging, it's important to take one section at a time rather than try to first survey a large area or an entire wall of the classroom.

You must first assess the spaces within your room. How do you do this? You need to look separately at each space within an area. With purging, it's important to take one section at a time (for example, a cabinet, a set of shelves, a corner of the room) rather than try to first survey a large area or an entire wall of the classroom. Looking at a smaller area first can help you avoid becoming overwhelmed by the project. Some people are surprised at how efficient it can be to focus on one single shelf, or perhaps one drawer of a file cabinet, at a time. It makes the overall process so much easier. After you have a handle on smaller areas, you can move toward organizing larger spaces, but for most people, starting smaller is definitely best in assessing your classroom spaces.

I usually take some notes as I walk or tour the spaces in the classroom. There are several important questions to ask yourself when assessing needs, but two key questions when touring any space include, "What is working in this space?" and "What is not working in the space?" Answering these questions first gives you a greater understanding of your desires for the spaces within your classroom.

Be sure to give yourself credit for the organizational systems that you already have in place, and don't change the systems that already work for you. As the saying goes, "Don't make changes for change's sake." For some guidance with this step, use the Assessing Classroom Spaces Sheet on page 207 in the appendix. This sheet is full of guiding questions that can help you identify how you want each space in your room to look and function so you will know which materials to purge and which to keep.

> Be sure to give yourself credit for the organizational systems that you already have in place, and don't change the systems that already work for you.

One area you may need to organize is a reading nook. What is currently working with the nook? Is it the layout, the furniture, or the shelving for the books? Now ask yourself what is not working in the reading area. Is it the system for returning books to the shelves, or perhaps the lighting? Is it too crowded?

Another area you may need to organize is a teacher cabinet. What do you feel you've organized well in this cabinet? Is your paper supply stored here? Do you have a good system for this? Are you storing necessary items within? Are you making good use of the space for supplies? Are you storing things properly in containers? Also consider what is not working for you. Is the cabinet cluttered? Is it neat and tidy? Do all of the items have a home, or are they randomly scattered about? Can you locate what you need, or do you have trouble finding supplies or materials when you open the cabinet?

TAKING STOCK

After assessing needs within your classroom, the next step is to take stock of what you own in the way of materials, such as office supplies as well as curriculum materials. This means being methodical about counting or at least getting a rough estimate of what you have. I keep a list of basic necessities, and each year I determine what items on this list I will need to replenish before the new school year. Here's my list of basic necessities:

- Paper clips
- Binder clips
- Correction fluid
- Staples
- Flip chart markers
- Overhead markers
- Dry-erase markers
- Ballpoint pens
- Mechanical pencils
- Chart paper
- Clear tape
- Masking tape
- Desk name tags

I keep a running record of my needs so I don't purchase items I already have. Lots of duplicate items contribute to clutter, which is the very thing you want to avoid in your quest to becoming more organized.

You might want quick results, so it may seem a little tedious to go through the process of first assessing your needs and taking stock of what you already have in your classroom, but both of these tasks are crucial to effectively using your resources and avoiding future clutter. Assessing your needs helps you identify the exact items you need in your classroom. It tells you what will be useful in your room and what will be clutter. Taking stock of what you have shows you the useful items you already have and reveals items you need to add to your classroom. It also shows you the items

Assessing your needs helps you identify the exact items you need in your classroom.

you have that you don't need—your current clutter. It's a backward process, thinking about end results before you physically purge, but it's a process that will help you to reach your goals! Use the Supplies Inventory Checklist on page 208 in the appendix to help you brainstorm ideas for your own list of basic necessities.

SORTING

The third step in the purging process is to sort your items into categories. There are many ways to approach this step. Simpler is better. A simple approach limits your choices and keeps things from becoming confusing. Confusion leads to undue stress and frustration, which may make you want to give up on the process. Simple means you sort one area at a time. The area could be as small as a shelf or a drawer. Remember, working in small sections keeps the task manageable. Simple also means you have the fewest number of categories necessary. To sort, I recommend you use a large bin or basket, or perhaps even large trash bags, for each category. That way you can keep track of all of the items as you are sorting. Be sure you have enough space to spread out as you are sorting, whether you sort on a large table or a section of the floor. Lack of space can contribute to frustration with the process. The basic categories for sorting are toss/trash, donate, and keep.

Toss/Trash

The toss/trash category is for those items that are broken, dirty, old, have missing pieces, or are outdated. Be honest when selecting items for the trash pile. I try to avoid telling people what items are best suited for this pile, but I do like to make suggestions when I know it is in their best interest. The trash pile should be obvious; it's for objects you don't use now, and no one else would be able to use them either.

Donate

The donate pile is for items that are in good shape but do not serve a purpose in your room. Promise yourself that you will be honest when sorting items, and only keep items that are truly useful or beneficial for running a successful classroom. To hold on to lots of miscellaneous items will only promote a sense of clutter in the long run. Try to make the sorting process as productive as possible.

If you need motivation to donate items, think of how excited the other teachers in your building will be to see your bounty of goodies when you set out the items for grabs. (It is sometimes comical the way we gravitate toward other teachers' discards, isn't it? I'm guilty of it myself, but as a side note, I recommend that you only take items from others' discards when you are 100 percent sure—okay, maybe 99.9 percent sure—you will use the items in your classroom. The item should help meet one of the needs you identified in your classroom space assessment or furniture consideration planning.)

> To hold on to lots of miscellaneous items will only promote a sense of clutter in the long run.

If you find that you need an item after donating it, you can usually borrow from another teacher during the current year, and then you can ultimately decide to put that item on your necessities list for the following year.

Keep

As the name implies, the keep pile is for all of the objects that will stay in your classroom. With purging, it can sometimes become difficult to make decisions about some of your items. When you assess an item and are unsure whether you should discard or donate the item, it's often a good idea to take some time to think on it further. Think about the item, and identify exactly how it might be useful. Specifically, if you can name at least one or two ways in which you might use the item in a subject area or within a curricular unit in your classroom, then by all means, keep it, being sure to store it properly (more about storage options in Chapter 4), and move on to the next item. However, if you come across an item and are muttering to yourself that "it could be useful ... somehow ... sometime..." without really going into specifics, your uncertainty indicates that it is probably not a "keep" item. Honesty is key in this stage.

GUIDELINES FOR KEEPING ITEMS

As you are sorting, you may come across items that you're not sure you'll use this year, but you have a strong feeling you will use at some time. Or maybe you find a resource you've had for a while and you're not sure how much longer you should keep it. How long is too long to keep things? Lots of organizing books suggest specific time frames for keeping items. If you really haven't used an item in a certain period of time, why hang on to it? I generally agree with this philosophy. I've found it true in the classroom, but with some varied exceptions. I use a helpful acronym when dealing with how long to save items in the classroom. We need to ROLL with our clutter! What does this mean?

Repeats
The *R* in ROLL stands for *repeats*. Carefully consider the number of repeat items that you store in your classroom. It's perfectly acceptable (and often advantageous) to keep more than one item in stock in your room in order to be well prepared for your daily instruction. For instance, you can never have too much correction fluid or too many paper clips or dry-erase markers, can you? But for the most

part, you need to keep items in check. Following the guidelines in the assess step of purging should keep you on track. If you have more copies than you need, it's best to put those items in the donate pile so another teacher can enjoy them.

Outdated

The *O* in ROLL stands for *outdated*. We often have trouble letting go of materials, because at some point in our teaching career, the materials in question had been useful, and it's hard for us to imagine letting go of something that had a purpose, even if it was some time ago. However, we need to be realistic about an item's current purpose. Think critically about the item. Will you actually use this item or these materials in a timely fashion? If you don't think you'll use an outdated item in question within a year, you need to let go of it. You'll be much happier in letting it go. It's one less piece of clutter in your classroom.

Level

The first *L* in ROLL stands for *level*. Carefully consider if the item in question will truly serve a purpose in your current grade level. If you know for a fact, pending any major changes in years to come, that you are truly an intermediate teacher, and you have lots of materials for primary grades, then pass those on to the kindergarten or first-grade teachers in your building. They'll love getting some super materials for their classrooms! By purging the items that are not useful at your grade level, you've helped to make more room for things you currently need.

I know teachers who hold on to materials for a very long time, and when I ask them why, they say that these materials hold special memories for them. If this is the case for you, decide what items are truly important for you, and perhaps create a memory box of teaching materials that will help memorialize those early teaching years. Then you can donate the rest of the items to others.

Love It

The last *L* in ROLL stands for *love it*. This is not a new descriptor for making decisions about purging, but it is such an important one when dealing with classroom materials. If you don't love the items in question, meaning they don't hold much value for you in enriching your yearly curriculum, then they are standing in your way as clutter.

I've sometimes had people tell me that they wanted to dispose of their clutter, but they never really took the time to deal with it. What better time than now to start making those decisions on your way to cutting the clutter!

So, in purging your classroom, always remember to ROLL with your clutter, and soon your classroom will be organized and clutter-free!

ROLL With Your Clutter

As you purge, use the acronym ROLL to evaluate items.

- R = **Repeats.** Do you have a lot of repeat items? Do you really need lots of one item?

- O = **Outdated.** Are your materials current? Do you use them regularly from year to year?

- L = **Level.** Do the materials and manuals you have match the grade level(s) you teach?

- L = **Love it.** Do you like, enjoy, and appreciate the value of each item in your classroom (such as supplies, books, teacher resource guides, etc.)?

Grade-Level Considerations

Elementary

All teachers, but especially elementary teachers, have multiple areas to purge within their classrooms. With cabinets full of student supplies, teacher resources, and multitudes of files, you must work from a model that emphasizes a small-to-large philosophy. This means you need to take on one area at a time and tackle it in stages. Think only about how that space should function. Of course, from time to time, it will be necessary to go to a different part of the room to put materials in other places, or perhaps bring other things into the space you are currently organizing, but don't make the mistake of trying to look at the forest first—meaning the whole room—and tearing through the entire space in one sitting. You'll end up exhausted and may decide to give up before you make any real progress in your classroom. Focusing on one space at a time is truly beneficial in organizing many areas within an elementary classroom.

Middle/High School

Middle school and high school teachers have much to consider in keeping files organized and tidy—perhaps even more than other grade-level teachers because of the number of students you see each day. Be sure to start with an area of high intensity, such as your filing system, early on in the organizing process. You have more energy when you're first starting an organizing project, and you'll need the initial higher energy level to work through intense sections of your room. It's important to do a thorough job with those spaces. Setting up, maintaining, and periodically purging your curricular and student files is crucial to keeping a well-ordered classroom. You'll find that once you tackle your filing system, you can move on to organizing other areas of the classroom with greater ease. You can find more specific tips and information on how to organize files in Chapter 7.

TEMPORARY CHAOS TO CREATE ORDER

A school colleague and I once sorted lots of papers and teacher resources together. As we worked, we began to place things around the room in different piles, and before long, we had created quite a spectacle of stuff around the room. It is important to remember that sorting and purging is messy work. Often, during the process of purging, you might begin to panic a bit, thinking that you are making a bigger mess of things than they were before you started the process! It really can become a bit daunting if you don't know what to expect. But, as I told my colleague, you need to allow for temporary chaos to create order. When you understand this and realize it for what it is during the actual process, you can remain calm, and keep at the task at hand, which is effective and efficient sorting and purging. Things may appear out of control, but if you are working methodically with clear sorting piles, you should be able to restore order quickly. And never underestimate the power of working in one small area at a time. It will limit the temporary chaos. Purging one section at a time can give you the confidence you need to work on another area of your classroom.

LEVELS OF PURGING

Let's face it, purging is hard work. Most of us don't enjoy the process. Purging can be both physically and emotionally draining, so it is definitely a process to be reckoned with. It's something for which we must prepare and plan carefully. All of this is true, but you need to repeat the purging process throughout the year. Regular purging causes your organizing systems to thrive by clearing away clutter. But don't think you need to do a major overhaul and tear everything apart once a month to purge. There are different levels of purging.

Surface Purging

Surface purging involves clearing or cleaning off surfaces and dealing with residual papers, notes, and reminders that you no longer need. You need to surface purge the items on your desk and work spaces on a daily basis so things don't start to pile up and clutter the spaces around the room.

Seasonal Purging

The next level of purging is seasonal purging. Every season (or quarter or semester), you should tour your room and think through your materials and supplies, making judgments about items you regularly use. These items might include actual seasonal items, such as decorations, posters or personal items, but they can also include curricular materials or supplies. Often I sort and purge items in my file cabinet during a seasonal purging to keep files orderly.

Deep-Clean Purging

The next level, the deepest level, is a thorough cleaning and purging process. I recommend you do this at least once per year. This process is the most exhaustive, and although it doesn't always involve throwing out great piles of things, it does entail some thoughtful reflection so you can identify the items you do not need and add them to the trash can or recycling bin. This is often the most rewarding level of purging, although it tends to be the most rigorous.

> Regular purging causes your organizing systems to thrive by clearing away clutter.

MAINTAINING CONTROL

How do you maintain control with purging? If you take time to assess what you want from your classroom spaces and then take stock of what you have in your classroom, you can dig into the purging process by following the steps listed in this chapter. The key is consistency and sticking with the process. Do surface purging daily. Keep up with seasonal purging, and try to accomplish one deep-clean purge per year. Happy purging!

The Positives of Purging

☐ Purging your spaces of items you no longer need or use can go a long way toward helping you become more organized.

☐ Purging is a key step toward long-term goals for organization.

☐ Purging gives you a feeling of being more in control of your spaces.

☐ Purging helps you feel confident and proud of what you own.

☐ Purging can help you put more value on the things you own, because in keeping an item, you are saying that it is worthy of your attention.

☐ Purging is not just about throwing things away; it's about thinking critically about what you do own and putting pride into those items.

☐ Purging can be done in stages and in small areas so it is not overwhelming.

4: Storage

"Out of clutter, find
simplicity. From discord,
find harmony. In the
middle of difficulty lies
opportunity."

— Albert Einstein

Finding appropriate storage options for our student materials, supplies, teacher resources, and plain old "stuff" can be downright maddening! But, in the words of Einstein, we can remain positive and find opportunity in this challenge. One of the most important considerations in achieving a calm, well-ordered classroom is to think carefully about aspects of storage. Finding proper storage often begins with considering the shelving and storage areas available to you. Before you go out and buy lots of colorful, unique storage containers, it is sensible and smart to consider whether these containers will fit into the storage areas you have and whether they are purposeful and functional as well. It is also important to measure your storage areas carefully for different types of storage containers. But first, you need to consider *what it is* you need to contain.

> One of the most important considerations in achieving a calm, well-ordered classroom is to think carefully about aspects of storage.

STUDENT SUPPLIES

How do we contain all of those student materials and supplies? As teachers, we know from experience (or, if you are a new teacher, you'll find out soon enough) how student materials can virtually take over our classrooms if we are not careful. Storing student supplies is a top priority in keeping your classroom organized. Most teachers already have lots of great ideas for containing student supplies, and there is no single correct way to store them. Many storage decisions for this category depend on the grade level you teach, as well as your personal preference for style, color, and type of materials. Because student materials vary so much, I've listed some specific suggestions by age range to give you some targeted ideas for storage.

Primary Grades

Primary teachers might want to house often-used student materials in colorful, small plastic caddies (with handles in the middle for carrying). When it comes time to use these materials, you can place them on student tables. This helps to promote a sense of organization as well as sharing among students. Having materials such as scissors, glue sticks, pencils, markers, and similar supplies all in one spot gives students immediate access to items they need during lessons. This is often preferable because getting up to retrieve materials on their own is not a quick or efficient process for younger students. Sometimes primary students may have their own small school boxes in which to contain their own supplies, but it's a good idea to contain lots of community items on student tables or desks.

Upper Elementary Grades

Most students in the upper elementary grades are at an age where they need (and want) their own space to contain supplies. Many teachers appreciate the idea of designating a central location for the majority of supplies and then asking students to retrieve materials as needed. One common idea for upper elementary teachers is to provide students with basic plastic supply boxes (shoebox size) to contain their general school supplies. These supply boxes can be purchased from any major retail store, office supply store, or discount store. They are simple, economical, and relatively sturdy.

Many teachers use an organizing system to identify students' boxes. Rather than names, it's a good idea to label the supply boxes with student numbers. This system makes the boxes reusable from one year to the next. It's a good idea to put these supply boxes on a shelf above student lockers or cubby spaces so students can easily locate and access them. Alternatively, you can place student supply boxes in a central location, such as an easily accessible shelving unit in the classroom.

Middle/High School

Middle and high school students need quite a few supplies for a variety of classes. Teachers can promote a sense of organization by stocking some of these often-used materials in their classrooms. Students must carry quite a load of books, binders, and spiral notebooks from class to class, and they are rarely able to get to their lockers to gather and bring a whole host of supplies with them from period to period. I recommend that you invest in an adequate supply of materials that you require for your curriculum. Suggested items include markers, colored pencils, scissors, rulers, and glue. Other supplies will depend on the subject area you teach.

Another portable option for supplies is to ask each student to bring a zipper pouch designed to fit in a three-ring binder. These pouches are generally sturdy and can hold pencils, erasers, sticky notes, scissors, and highlighters. Students can bring these pouches from class to class, cutting down on the number of trips to lockers, as well as reducing the amount of supplies teachers need to purchase for their classrooms. This method can also be useful in upper elementary classrooms where students switch classes.

Borrow Boxes

Borrow boxes are useful for storing a variety of items and student materials. If you have extra pens, pencils, and other supplies, place them in containers in a central location in your classroom and allow students to borrow items as needed. Depending on your grade level or the subject(s) that you teach, you can adjust the borrow-box system in your classroom. Here are some guidelines for using them:

Explain expectations to students: It's important to explain specific expectations for these borrow boxes. Students need to understand that they are welcome to access the materials as needed, but they need to return the materials when they are finished using them. Reinforcing aspects of responsible behavior is always a good idea.

Label your boxes: It's easier to find various materials when they are labeled well. I use my Brother label machine to create simple labels to place on the shoebox-sized containers. Students can then locate what they need with ease.

Make use of end-of-the-year donations: Many times at the end of the year, kids don't want to keep a few markers or a partially used glue stick. A colleague of mine once suggested that we ask students not to throw out these used items, but rather to donate their unwanted materials to these borrow boxes. You'll be surprised how quickly your borrow boxes can fill at the end of a school year with gently used student leftovers!

I store my borrow items in bins on my shelving unit. I also have a small metal cart next to the borrow shelves. This cart has a few

Category Ideas for Borrow Boxes

- Scissors
- Sticky notes
- Highlighters
- Calculators
- Markers
- Colored pencils
- Crayons
- Clear tape refills
- Masking tape
- Rulers
- Protractors
- Glue/glue sticks
- Index cards

shelves with space for small items such as tape dispensers, staplers, hole punches, as well as things like felt-tip permanent markers and dry-erase markers. I like this open-cart concept because students can access these items quickly and easily. Having a hub for borrowed materials is key because students access these materials so frequently.

STUDENT DESKS

For elementary teachers, student desks are important storage areas for housing a large majority of student supplies. Here are some guidelines for helping students with storing items in their desks:

Smart Storage

Students will store most of their books, spiral notebooks, and binders in their desks. Take time to teach students some basic logic about how to store items. For instance, my grade-level team decided to ask students at my school to use binders for each class. It is difficult to get multiple binders into student desks, so it's a good idea to train students to alternate the directions of the binders. Teach students to store binders upside down on top of each other so they can maximize space within their desks by lining up a thin binder end with a thick binder end. You'd think students would know this, but you shouldn't assume they know all of the tricks of the trade, even if it seems logical.

Desk Alternatives

If students do not have desks, you will need to determine efficient storage solutions for students' supplies and materials. One idea for alternate storage is to use their mailbox slots. These are good locations for textbooks or other items of similar size. Students can easily access these items when they get ready to switch classes or when they are preparing to go home. In addition, some teachers allow for (or require) students to store textbooks or other like materials in a locker or cubby area. Providing students with alternate options for storage ensures that students are not constantly struggling with how to store (or cram!) items in their desks.

For students in middle and high school, it is standard practice for them to carry textbooks and other supplies back and forth from their lockers to classes each day. It is not usually feasible for teachers to house large numbers of textbooks in the classroom. If textbooks are not used daily or if individual students do not need to take them home each night, one alternate storage idea is to house a class set of students' textbooks on a shelf and ask students to retrieve them during lessons only when needed.

Provide Specific Expectations for Supplies

It's important for students to store specific supplies in their desk (in addition to textbooks, spiral notebooks, binders, etc.). This is an efficient time-saver for transitions between activities or lessons, or within a given lesson when you need students to get an item at a moment's notice. For instance, I usually ask that students keep at least one highlighter, an extra pencil or two, an eraser, and sometimes a ballpoint pen handy in their desks for various reading or writing tasks so they do not need to get up from their seats to retrieve items from their supply boxes, which can waste precious instructional time.

Manage Student Trinkets

It's important for teachers in any grade level to allow students *some* say as to what they'd like to keep in their desks. This helps students feel that they can personalize their space and gives them some comfort during the day. (Think of the personal items teachers bring to school to accomplish this same purpose.) Students of all ages sometimes like to keep small toys or fun pencil sharpeners or other items in their desks. I don't mind this practice, on two conditions:

1. The trinkets or items themselves cannot become a distraction.

2. Students may not store large numbers of such items in their desks.

When students' desks are full of these items, the healthy sense of order in the room can be disrupted, and the trinkets often become a source of clutter—not to mention that toys often are a distraction to other students who enter the classroom and sit at these desks when switching classes.

> It's important for teachers in any grade level to allow students some say as to what they'd like to keep in their desks.

TEACHER STORAGE AREAS

When storing large quantities of teaching items, such as curricular materials, paper, teacher resource guides, or other necessary materials, it is important to consider the current spaces you have in your classroom and then plan for efficient ways to organize these materials. Here are some suggestions for various storage areas you might have around your classroom:

Storage Cabinets

Most teachers have some type of storage cabinet for supplies and materials. Carefully plan what items to place within the cabinets and plan how to organize these cabinets. If you haphazardly toss items in your cabinets, you will no doubt experience a sense of stress because it will likely be cluttered and messy, making it difficult to find anything later. Here are some considerations for storing items in these cabinets:

Consider your needs: Think about the items you need to contain in your classroom. Do you have a large number of materials for a specific subject? It is likely that you will need to devote some of your storage cabinet space to these materials. Do you have a large number of teacher resource manuals or idea books? If so, the cabinet may be an important place to store them.

Contain loose items: Don't put loose items into the cabinet. They will either get scattered and lost or will take up too much surface space. If you have loose items, put them in a container before placing them in the cabinet. If you have loose papers, put them in a folder. If you have loose folders, put them in a binder. Do you have lots of dry-erase markers, pens, and other supplies? Put them in a shoe-box-sized container. Do you have lots of holiday classroom decorations? (First, be sure that you truly use these decorations and that they are in good shape—not faded, ripped, or have seen better days!) Store them in small plastic containers (with labels) in your storage cabinet so these decorations are portable and well protected.

Create zones: If you have a variety of items in your cabinets, create zones for each type of material. A zone could be an entire cabinet, one or two shelves, or even half a shelf if it is a small category. Labels can help you remember zones and make it quick to find materials.

Be sure that no matter what you place in any storage cabinet in your classroom, you have carefully planned what to store there and how to store it properly. The most important thing is to avoid tossing items inside the cabinets willy-nilly with an out-of-sight, out-of-mind attitude. The clutter will still be looming, and you will need to contain it properly to achieve a sense of order. And, as I emphasized in Chapter 3, I recommend purging your storage cabinets once a year. It is an important step in keeping your classroom well organized, and it helps to ensure that the materials and resources you have are indeed useful for instruction, current, and in good shape. Plus, each time you purge your cabinet, you are making room for more great items to store!

> The most important thing to avoid when placing items in storage cabinets is tossing items inside the cabinets willy-nilly with an out-of-sight, out-of-mind attitude. The clutter will still be looming, and you will need to contain it properly to achieve a sense of order.

Shelving Units

You can store just about anything you have in your classroom on shelves. Again, it's important to plan out your space and decide what you need to store. How you utilize this space depends on your personal preferences as well as the grade level(s) and the subject area(s) you teach. Here are some specific examples of how you might use shelves within your room:

Classroom libraries: Teachers who have classroom libraries (in any grade level) absolutely need shelving space to contain their books. It is critical to decide how to house the books themselves. Be sure to determine (or at least estimate) how much shelving space is needed for your library of books, and be realistic about storage possibilities if you find you don't have enough shelving space for your existing books. See Chapter 5 for specific tips for maintaining class libraries.

Curriculum materials: Teachers who use a variety of lab materials or hands-on items for lessons need to be creative in storing items on shelves. You can keep some of these items in a storage cabinet if one is available. If you have a grade-level workroom or other storage location (such as a science lab), store items in these spaces first so you have more available space on the shelves in your room for other items. Here are some questions that will be helpful in determining the best storage options for curriculum supplies:

- What supplies or materials do you need to contain?
- What type of container will work best?
- How many containers will you need?
- Can you store the containers on shelves, in a cabinet, or in another location?
- Are all supplies and materials current, not expired, and safe for student use?
- Do you want to store curricular materials on your shelves designated for teacher use only, or do you want to allow students to access the shelves during lessons?

One consideration is to clearly label all bins, containers, or boxes so they are easy to access. In terms of storage options themselves, I recommend clear bins or containers so you can see the materials inside without opening the lid. Always think of how to make your life easier, if only a little bit, with each small decision regarding storage solutions in your classroom.

Teacher resource books and manuals: Shelving units are ideal places for storing all of your resource books and teacher manuals. These books are critical to your instruction and need to be contained properly on shelving near your teacher work area. For specific information about how to organize your teacher resource books and manuals, see Chapter 8.

Student binders: Many teachers, from upper elementary through high school, choose to have students use binders to store and carry papers for various content areas or from class to class. If students do not need to bring their binders to and from class each day, and if you have the storage space available, it can be helpful to designate some shelving space for storing students' binders. This approach is especially helpful for elementary classrooms in order to free up storage space inside desks. It also prevents middle and high school students from having to carry excess supplies with them from class to class.

Although there are many more uses for shelving within the classroom, these examples give you an idea of how to think creatively about storing various items. Remember that there is no right or wrong way to store materials and supplies. Storage decisions depend on your style and preference, and will vary depending on your grade level and curriculum needs. The key is to be thoughtful and plan ahead. That way, your storage systems do not appear cluttered or confusing. As with cabinets, breaking shelves down into zones and labeling each zone can help you maintain your organizing system. You and your students will know where to find materials and how to store them properly.

Crates and Bins

Plastic bins are a teacher's best friend. They come in so many sizes and colors, and they can be used for a number of purposes in the classroom. One of the best ways to use bins is in storing your classroom library books. Another idea is to use bins to contain teacher resource materials. In years past, I've organized teacher resource books and manuals in plastic bins by subject area and stored them on a shelving unit near my desk. When I needed to pull a resource book by subject area, I knew exactly where it was. Keep in mind that you'll likely need adjustable shelves to accommodate plastic crates.

When we don't have sufficient shelving due to budget constraints or other reasons, we need to get creative about effective ways to store materials. For instance, I have used standard plastic crates, stacked one on top of the other, to house student binders for my language arts classes. These binders are important parts of my classroom routine, but students do not need to carry them back and forth each day, so I decided to place them on my back counter in the crates. This system allows students to retrieve their binders from the crates for daily lessons.

Crates can also be useful for storing a variety of student work. I use a crate to house student writing workshop pieces. Each student has a manila folder within a hanging file folder in the writing crate, and the students put in and take out their writing workshop pieces throughout the year. This idea can be easily modified for any subject area in which students need to store papers or projects in the classroom. Crates are more open and easier to access than filing cabinets.

Remember that there is no right or wrong way to store materials and supplies. Storage decisions depend on your style and preference, and will vary depending on your grade level and curriculum needs. The key is to be thoughtful and plan ahead.

STORING TEACHER MATERIALS

Here are options for storing your teaching supplies:

Seasonal Storage

There are lots of ways to store seasonal items. For flat decorations, such as posters or bulletin boards sets, most teachers use some sort of prefabricated cardboard storage box, which can be found in any teacher store. These generally fit most sizes of posters and decorations, and also have dividers, which can be purchased as needed. I like using these types of organizers because you truly do need something rather large to contain all of these items. For actual holiday decorations, such as lights, stuffed animals, and holiday toys, it is best to use clear plastic bins to contain these items. Tuck them away in your storage cabinet or on a shelf out of view. These items need

Other Uses for Crates and Bins

- Make a lost-and-found bin and place it in an easily accessible place in the classroom.

- Gather books for an "Author of the Month" or "Illustrator of the Month" bin. Students will be exposed to a new author or illustrator each month and may find some great reads!

- Store student-made books or writing pieces in bins and label it "Classroom Authors."

- Store multiple clipboards in crates.

- Store small dry-erase whiteboards in crates or bins.

to be accessed at only specific times of the school year, and if not housed properly, they can become distractions or visual clutter.

Charts and Posters

You will likely not put up every single chart or poster you own on the walls of your classroom at the same time, so you will need a good storage container to house unused posters and charts. As I do for holiday posters or bulletin boards, I use cardboard storage boxes for posters and charts. It is essential to use an efficient storage system for these items. Other options are available as well such as large, clear plastic carriers. These often have sturdy plastic handles, and they allow you to easily transport posters around the room. The one drawback to these plastic storage carriers is that they do not hold as many posters or charts. They are handy when you don't have many items to store. Another idea is to use storage holders or carriers with hooks, which allow you to hang the containers on the wall, chalkboard, or white board. This helps to keep things off the floor and keeps clutter from collecting around the room.

Construction Paper and Stationery

Most teachers have some use for construction paper, colored paper, or stationery. It's sometimes a struggle to figure out how to contain paper. Depending on how much you have, it can be tricky to find suitable storage options. I am fortunate to have a storage cabinet in my room, and I use it to store all of my paper. I can stack the paper neatly by color on different shelves. Construction paper goes on one shelf, and colored paper and stationery go on another shelf. I can locate what I need at a moment's notice. For those teachers who do not have a storage cabinet, or for those who want their paper supplies more easily accessible, you can use plastic storage drawer units to contain paper. For instance, you might store all of your construction paper separated by color in one or two plastic storage drawer units stacked on a shelf in the classroom. You can also store your colored copy paper and stationery in the same manner. The key when storing paper this way is to be sure to use your handy label machine. Labeling these drawers ensures that students (and teachers!) put paper in the proper locations.

For other teachers, storing paper neatly on a shelf works just fine, but be careful when storing paper in this manner because it may become messy. Also, if students are not given clear expectations regarding using paper and maintaining order, you will need to find an alternate storage method to keep your paper supply organized.

Resource Books

Teachers have a variety of resources to store in the classroom. You might need to store books such as dictionaries, thesauruses, atlases, and class sets of textbooks. Think about where to store these resources so you can easily locate them. Making smart decisions about where to house your resource materials will help you plan effectively for instruction.

I usually incorporate several copies of these resources in my room because I want students to become familiar with using them as additional ways to manage and retrieve information for a variety of projects or assignments. Although students are becoming increasingly adept at using the Internet for finding information (such as online dictionaries and scores of articles about topics of interest), it is a good idea to direct students toward locating information in traditional types of resources so they are well rounded in seeking out facts, ideas, and research. Here are some tips for storing these resources:

Use countertop spaces. If you have access to counter space in your classroom, you might decide to store various resources on these countertops. You can place the books directly on the countertops using bookends. If there's space, containing the resources in bins or crates on your counters makes them more portable, should students need to take them to different parts of the classroom for activities or projects. Using counters in these ways ensures that you use the space more efficiently. It also eliminates (or at least reduces the chance for) the accumulation of clutter throughout the classroom.

Use portable carts. If you have access to metal rolling carts or something similar, you may find them helpful for storing these bulky resources. The portability is nice, too, in case you need to share resources with another teacher or if you want to store these resources in a different location, perhaps in a teacher work room or other resource room space, when not in use.

Miscellaneous Supplies

Teachers of all grade levels often have lots of miscellaneous supplies throughout the classroom. We usually have a purpose for them (especially if we have gone through the important steps of purging), but where do we store all of these items?

Cleaning supplies: Depending on your school district, you may need to follow certain health codes for storing cleaning supplies to keep them away from students. Even so, it is important that you have certain cleaning supplies on hand, especially cleaning wipes for student desks, tables, and other surfaces around the classroom. Locate a cubby or a spot high on a shelf or in a storage cabinet that you can devote to storing cleaning supplies. You may want to put cleaning supplies in a plastic tub or caddy for portability.

Plastic baggies: Most teachers use plastic baggies in various sizes (snack, sandwich, quart, and gallon) to contain materials. Baggies serve a multitude of purposes, from storing small items such as beads and buttons, to holding game pieces, activity cards, and student novels. For whatever purpose you use them, you'll need a place to store baggies, especially if you have each of your students bring in a box at the beginning of the year. I've found that baggies store well under a sink (if you have one in your room) or on a shelf above student lockers or cubbies. They stack easily, and students can access them when needed.

Tissues: Where would we be without tissues? It's amazing how many we go through each year. Tissue boxes are bulky, but they stack

Surefire Storage Tips

Do

- ☐ Determine what you need to contain.
- ☐ Carefully measure the space in which you want to store items. Buy containers that will fit these spaces.
- ☐ Buy sturdy containers, especially for heavier items.
- ☐ Label your containers.
- ☐ Store often-used materials and supplies at a lower level. Store less-often used supplies higher up on shelves.
- ☐ Purge the items in your storage containers at least once a year. Determine if any items are expired, outdated, ripped, or not used in the current curriculum. Toss them, donate them to another teacher, or recycle them (if able).
- ☐ Be willing to change your storage options if they are not working for you. Sometimes you can only know what works for you if you are first willing to try one option for a while. If it doesn't work, try another option. If money is an object, live with your storage solutions for a year or two, and then determine and plan accordingly for what could work more efficiently the following year.

easily. Store tissues wherever you have extra space. I typically keep tissues above my student locker/cubby area or on one side of my teacher cabinet.

Don't

- ☐ Don't assume that a fellow colleague's storage system will work for you—each of us is different in our style, our preferences, the materials we need to contain, and our ability to make systems work.

- ☐ Don't give up if one idea doesn't work for you; be willing to try a plan B.

- ☐ Don't make your storage options so complicated that students won't know how to properly access them.

- ☐ Don't buy lots of containers before determining your storage needs. This is a common mistake that many of us make.

- ☐ Don't buy containers that are cumbersome or bulky.

5: Organizing the Classroom Zones

"It's one thing not to see the forest for the trees, but then to go on to deny the reality of the forest is a more serious matter."

— Paul Weiss

Many teachers find the prospect of organizing their classrooms daunting when they look at it as a whole. When we stand just inside our rooms and see it as a whole, it can be difficult to know where to begin to organize the spaces within. It's helpful to think of the "forest for the trees" analogy here. In efficiently planning for organizing and maintaining order in our classrooms, we need to think about the room as a whole unit to get a general picture of how we want it to look and function. But to successfully store and manage our supplies, materials, and other items, it is important to think about spaces within the room—specific zones. Read on to discover ways to organize these areas of your classroom. When you focus on these spaces one by one, you'll be on your way to a well-ordered, functional, and purposeful classroom.

ZONE ONE: THE TEACHER'S DESK

I start with the teacher's desk because this area is a key to organizing our most-used items. The teacher's desk is the hub of a teacher's realm. Some teachers don't use a formal desk and instead prefer tables of various sizes or even just a small student desk from which to work. I personally appreciate the space afforded with a teacher's desk and the accompanying drawers—all of which help me contain my essential supplies—but your personality (and sometimes space restrictions) will dictate your preferences. It's important to understand that there is not a universally acknowledged correct type of desk to use.

Whatever type of teacher's desk you use, you'll need to discover organizational balance, or you run the risk of accumulating clutter and making your life more stressful on a day-to-day basis. Let's look at the different sections of the teacher's desk.

Fingertip Items

One of my clients wondered about what to do to change the look of her classroom desk so it was more streamlined and clutter-free. The first thing I asked her was, "Well, what items do you need at your fingertips?" This discussion helped us determine which items needed to stay on or in her desk permanently so she could access them at a moment's notice, thereby making her day-to-day work a little easier.

The first step in considering the organization of your desktop and drawers is to consider what you need at your fingertips on a *daily* basis. Identify these items by homing in on those things you use frequently to do your job effectively.

Of course, fingertip items will vary from teacher to teacher and from grade level to grade level, but for the most part, there are usually some essentials to consider, such as:

- Computer
- Correction fluid
- Pens
- Pencils
- Calculator
- Clear tape
- Scissors
- Stapler
- Sticky notes
- Paper clips
- Binder clips
- Lesson plans

Desktop

How will you store items on top of your desk? It is often important to store a variety of paperwork (files, folders, memos, and more) on your desk so you can easily access what you need. Chapter 7 is full of tips and information about how to handle aspects of paperwork. Here I also want to mention the importance of having a paper sorter or file sorter on your desk. This sorter can act as a hub for important day-to-day paperwork. Use manila folders and designate categories for your paperwork.

Some possible categories for folders include:

- Memos
- Action File
- To File
- To Copy
- To Grade

To keep your desk clean and organized, it's important to maintain order on a consistent basis. You need to keep your desk free from clutter so you can stay focused and calm during otherwise busy days. How do we do this when our days are so busy? Remember the surface-level purging tips from Chapter 3. Do some surface-level purging on your desktop every day or two. You may only move loose papers into your paperwork hub and recycle papers you no longer need. If you do it daily, it will take less than five minutes. You can spare five minutes in exchange for a clear desktop at the end of each day, right? For ideas on how to find time daily to surface-level purge see the "Planning for Tomorrow" section (page 149) in Chapter 11.

Drawers

If you use a desk with drawers, organize them well so they do not become a catchall for a variety of supplies. A catchall is a difficult thing to avoid because we don't always have time on a day-to-day basis to micro-organize every single thing that finds its way inside the drawers. Many times, when pulling out a drawer and seeing miscellaneous dice, game pieces, or other odds and ends, I've asked myself, "How did that get in there?" or even, "What is this used for?" Oftentimes, we toss things in our desks without much thought to organizing because in the moment we simply don't have the time to think about the item.

To organize drawers well, there are several things to consider:

- Plan uses for the drawers ahead of time. Determine the most logical and convenient places for storing items you use on a daily basis. Think about the size of each drawer and what items will best fit within those spaces. Assign certain items to specific drawers. For instance, I've designated a drawer in my desk for only paper clips, binder clips, staples, and other similar items. Place like items together. This careful preplanning helps you to quickly locate supplies in the future. Having a plan and placing supplies with careful forethought promotes a sense of order and calm in your surroundings.

- If applicable, use drawer organizers to further organize your desk. A variety of types are available, and many are adjustable so you do not need to be as particular about measuring to fit the space. Drawer organizers give clarity about what to contain; they provide shape and structure. They allow you to store several different types of items in separate areas of a single drawer. Additionally, when you place items in organizers, this allows for portability in moving things to different locations in the classroom if need be.

- To ensure that your desk drawers stay organized, I recommend that you clean them out at least twice a year. I go drawer by drawer and take everything out, determining what I need and use. Everything else goes in the donation or trash piles. Taking the time to purge drawers of unnecessary items helps minimize the chance for clutter, allowing you to use only those items that you really need.

ZONE TWO: THE LIBRARY

There are many great resources exclusively dedicated to helping teachers better organize their classroom libraries on the market. (A brief list of helpful resources can be found in the appendix within the Suggested Reading List.) A well-organized classroom library will help your students get the best benefits for their reading experiences. For elementary teachers, this is especially important. If you're a middle school teacher, you likely have a variety of books housed within your classrooms as well, depending on your subject area. If you're a high school teacher, you have many resources that you need to organize, although you may not need to house scores of novels and other books. Here are a few helpful ways to think about organizing a classroom library:

Methods for Organizing and Maintaining Books

Use bins and tubs: There are so many ways to organize your classroom library books, but using tubs and bins is extremely helpful in keeping a library organized for the long haul. Tubs or bins allow students easy access to books. They are also typically sturdy and cost effective. Shop around for good deals, and think about choosing a couple of different sized bins so they will be able to properly contain all of your books.

Choose logical categories: How you organize your classroom books will vary. It is largely up to you and your personality style. Consider the following tips when thinking about organizing your library:

- Color coding
- Organize by genre
- Organize by series or topic
- Organize by author
- Organize with student input

Color coding: Some teachers rely on a color-coding system to indicate reading levels of books or to differentiate between genres. This type of system is sometimes helpful for younger students when they are not as able to choose books independently. By determining various levels for students and guiding them toward choosing certain books at their "just right" level, we can ensure that students are expanding their reading minds by selecting books they can read and enjoy.

Organize by genre: As an upper elementary teacher, I've found that it is efficient to organize my classroom library by genre. In so doing, I am easily able to promote different types of literature, and students can access the books independently as well.

When I first considered how to organize my classroom library years ago, I realized the importance of the task ahead. I knew that I needed to develop a system that would allow students to sign out and return books properly and easily. I also knew that my students' prior knowledge about determining proper book genres would vary from year to year. Because of this, I came to understand that students could have trouble initially in determining a book's genre. While part of my job as a reading teacher is to teach students how to independently determine book genres, I did not want that to be their primary concern. Rather, I wanted them to find great books that appealed to them. I wanted them to explore and choose a variety of books.

I decided to use a small rectangular label to identify the book by genre. As I acquire new books for my classroom library, I write a code on the label to indicate genre. For instance, if the book is a historical fiction title, I write "HF" on the label and place it on the top right-hand side of the book cover. If the book is realistic fiction, I'll write "RF" on the label. Many teachers find this to be an efficient way to manage and maintain their classroom libraries.

Organizing books by genre in this manner takes some time. During my first year of organizing books this way, a fellow colleague and I joined forces to help each other go through every single book in our growing class libraries and label all the books at once. It takes a bit of a planning and an initial time investment to organize a classroom library this way, but doing so saved time for me later in the school year, and it provided just what we wanted for our students in handling books: An efficient, simple way to browse, check out, and return books independently.

I've found that organizing by genre provides a structure by which kids can maintain order; they can independently replace books when they are finished with them, and the library itself rarely gets messy or out of hand because each book has a proper place. Students can manage the library area well with this organizational system.

Organize by series or topic: Another popular way to organize books is by series. Organizing books in this manner allows kids to go straight to the *Harry Potter* or *39 Clues* or *Charlie Bone* tubs and pick out what they want to read. Some teachers also like to organize by topic. This is especially helpful for primary teachers because students can find topics of immediate interest with little help from adults. Some examples are animal books, counting books, or shape and color books. Students can choose these books quickly when teachers organize in a structured way.

Organize by author: Primary and upper elementary teachers often organize their classroom library books by author as well, which is helpful when doing author studies or using books by different authors to demonstrate writing styles.

Abbreviations for Genres

If you group your books by genre and decide to label them accordingly, be sure to determine logical abbreviations that are easy for your students to remember. I like Fountas and Pinnell's general labeling system for books. Some (modified) examples include:

RF = Realistic Fiction

HF = Historical Fiction

M = Mystery

F = Fantasy

BIO = Biography

P = Poetry

Organize with student input: Many teachers elicit student suggestions for how to organize the classroom library. When students have input about how the library should be organized, they feel a sense of ownership. Students will be inspired to check out books because they played an active role in setting up an organizational system. This approach to organizing your library can take a lot of additional time, especially if you already have a system that is up and running from the previous year. It can take up time that students would otherwise have for active reading experiences. Many teachers feel, however, that this is a great way to motivate students for reading. As an alterative, you may want to set up a system that you feel is sound and then invite students to make some minor adjustments to the library setup as the year progresses. This way, students are actively involved, and they have some ownership in how the library is organized.

Checking Out Books

To maintain an organized classroom library, your students need to know how to properly take out and return books. Students can check out books in a variety of ways. Some teachers use a system with an index card box and index cards. Each book has a pocket containing an index card, and students check out books by writing their name and the date on the card and then placing it under an index card divider.

Another way to set up a checkout system is to use a simple sign-out sheet. This is the system I use. On this sheet, students enter book information such as title and author, as well as the student's name, the date checked out, the date checked in, and the teacher's initials. I ask students to involve me in the book checkout process by bringing me the clipboard so I can sign off on the book that they turn in. This way, I not only know for sure that they put the books back where they belong, but I also have a working knowledge about what my students are reading.

Some teachers do not use any checkout system for books. This is a personal decision. Asking students to sign out books promotes personal responsibility, as well as a sense of respect about borrowing and returning materials. Whatever your checkout system, be sure you can remain consistent with the process so your classroom library continues to function well and remain organized.

ZONE THREE: THE COMPUTER AREA

Most teachers have access to one or more computers in their classrooms. If you have only one computer, then organizing this space should be relatively easy to manage. Consider placing the computer against a wall, and ensure that the computer is easy to access from different parts of the classroom.

If you have more than one computer in the room, it's important to place computers in such a way that the computer cables and plugs are near outlets. If your school has computer tables, the placement of the computers is dictated by where the hookups are located.

Always initiate student responsibility for organizing this area. For instance, at the end of the day, ask students to properly cover the computers, push in the chairs or stools, and maintain the cleanliness of the tables. Also, be sure to keep keyboards clean by wiping them down with a damp (not wet!) wipe, and use a static-free cloth to clean monitors. Doing so ensures that students help take proper care of the classroom equipment, as well as cut down on germs.

ZONE FOUR: LOCKER/CUBBY AREAS

There are many configurations in schools for lockers. If you teach in an elementary setting, this section will likely be more useful to you than it will be for a middle or high school teacher (however, it's a great idea to teach and reinforce the following tips with middle and high school students as well). Within the elementary classroom, it is critical to keep these areas clean and free from clutter. Whether you have established lockers that close, such as metal lockers, or simply an open, built-in area with hooks for coats and book bags or backpacks, you will need to set up structures for organizing this space.

In the fall and winter, students will have lots of coats and accessories, but in the spring, it will be somewhat easier to maintain these areas. Whatever the season, here are some important considerations:

Make Students Aware of Your Expectations

If you expect students to house only certain items within their locker areas, be open and direct with them so they understand what you expect them to do. Don't assume students know what you want unless you give them parameters for your expectations. For instance, because the locker areas in my classroom are open built-ins, I do not like lots of binders, spiral notebooks, or loose papers cluttering the space. So, for the most part, the large section of the locker area is to remain clear. Other than the folder that they may leave behind, my students are to keep this area free from materials or supplies. I ask them to take their coats, jackets, sweaters, or accessories home each night so the area is clean and ready for the next day. In my classroom, there is a shelf directly above the locker/cubby area, which is the perfect place for my students to store their supply boxes. These supply boxes contain all of their main supplies that they need for the year.

Other teachers may have different expectations for their lockers, so whatever you desire for the look of your locker area space, be sure to communicate clearly with your students.

Follow Through

If you notice throughout a given day that coats are strewn on the floor or that backpacks are not on their appointed hooks, make it a weekly student job to restore order to the area. Determine if you want consequences or rewards for keeping the space well organized and clean. From year to year, you'll find that some classes are more naturally inclined than others in keeping this area clean, so you may have to adjust your plan for communicating and reinforcing expectations each school year. What worked for your locker area organization one year may change the next year. You may need to plan for some slight alterations the following year in how you guide students to keep these spaces clean.

Clean Frequently

It's important for students to clean out their lockers and supply boxes a couple of times per year. When you reinforce the idea of keeping the classroom spaces clean and well ordered, you accomplish two things. You provide an opportunity for students to learn the benefits of being responsible for their belongings, and you promote an eye for purging things as well. By purging, students get rid of items that are no longer useful, are broken, or are no longer needed. When asking students to organize and clean these areas, you are also promoting organizational habits that they can use after they leave your classroom.

From year to year, you'll find that some classes are more naturally inclined than others in keeping this area clean, so you may have to adjust your plan for communicating and reinforcing expectations each school year.

ZONE FIVE: THE SINK/COUNTER AREA

Though I mentioned counter areas previously, I still consider this a separate zone within the classroom. If you have a sink or counter area in your room, decide early on how you want to utilize this space. As with any classroom space, you need to be methodical in planning out how to store items. As mentioned above, any time you have built-in possibilities for storage, you should take advantage of it. You just need to decide what to store on your counter(s) and how to store it.

For a time, I stored some encyclopedias and other reference books on the counter in my room. It was not an ideal place for them because my actual classroom library was on the other side of the room. But I simply couldn't contain these resources on the shelves in my classroom; they took up too much space, and they crowded out room that I needed for my novels and picture books. I determined that I needed to store the reference books in a different part of the room. After considering my options, I decided to place them on the counter across from my student lockers. I was able to line up the books in an organized fashion, which made the space look clean and crisp. I later moved the encyclopedias to a cart on wheels, which helped with the portability and functionality of these items.

I've also stored student binders in crates on the countertops in my classroom. Students in my room need daily access to their reading binders, but I didn't have enough space on my existing shelving units for them. So I needed to get creative about housing them elsewhere in the classroom. I didn't want to rely on students to take these binders with them each day because they use them to record and organize a variety of activities we do during class. So utilizing the counter space was a helpful means to an organizational end.

ZONE SIX: GAME/RECESS MATERIALS

Although this section likely won't apply to teachers outside of the elementary school range, I would be remiss if I didn't mention the importance of keeping your recess games and materials organized.

Many teachers have designated storage cabinets or drawers somewhere in the classroom for these items. The key to storing recess materials is to place them where students can easily access them. Storing games on one of the top shelves of your room won't serve your students well (unless, of course, you've taken the games away from them!).

Sometimes teachers store recess items in bins or crates, especially if they do not have storage cabinets or drawers. It's important to label these items well if you want items to return to the same bin or crate. You can use a variety of storage possibilities for games. Plastic baggies can be used to contain small, loose pieces, such as checkers, dice, or other parts. Many retail stores have colorful plastic boxes that you can buy for the purpose of storing board games—a great idea for when the original game box rips. These game boxes are sturdy and will last a long time.

I recommend that you check your game area at least twice a year—once at the beginning of the year as you are preparing your room, and once at the end of the year as you are organizing your room for the summer. I also like to enlist student assistance midyear so that I can be sure that game pieces are in the appropriate places and that game boards are well organized on the cabinet shelves. If you ask students to do various jobs around the room, make a student responsible for checking recess games. This way, students can tidy and organize as needed, and monitor the game area regularly. I also recommend that you do a "game check" at least once a year, with students' help, to ensure that pieces are not missing, that games have batteries (if needed), and that the games you own are ones that students use. If I notice students are not using a particular game for a number of years, I donate it because it's just a source of clutter. Kids usually love to help with organizing recess game pieces, so take them up on it and initiate their help with this sometimes tedious task!

> Do a "game check" at least once a year, with students' help, to ensure that pieces are not missing, that games have batteries (if needed), and that the games you own are ones that students use.

Organize Your Classroom Zones

As the year progresses, you may feel a bit overwhelmed about keeping the classroom in order. It's a good idea to evaluate one section of your room at a time and consider whether the space is organized and is working for you. Here are some important tips to remember for keeping each classroom zone organized:

Teacher's Desk

☐ Clean out your desk at least twice a year.

☐ Make sure your fingertip items are easy to locate on or in your desk.

☐ Determine items that should be relocated to a different part of the room.

☐ Toss any miscellaneous items (or items that mysteriously appeared).

☐ Group like items together.

☐ Consider using drawer organizers.

☐ Determine appropriate items for each drawer in your desk so it makes sense to you.

Classroom Library

☐ Take time to think about and determine the best organizational system based on your preferences.

☐ Choose sturdy, appropriately sized bins or tubs for storage.

☐ Group books in logical ways (by genre, by author, or by topic).

☐ Maintain your library. Enlist student help, and ask students to organize the bins on a regular basis.

☐ Establish an effective book sign-out system. Communicate your expectations to students, and maintain it throughout the year.

Computer Area

☐ Determine an efficient organizational arrangement for computers. Place computers in locations close to outlets.

☐ Be sure computers are accessible and conducive to traffic flow.

- ☐ Clean computers regularly.
- ☐ Enlist student assistance in ensuring that student monitors are covered and chairs or stools are pushed in each day.

Locker/Cubby Area

- ☐ Determine your expectations for keeping this area organized.
- ☐ Communicate clearly with students about how you want them to organize and keep this space tidy.
- ☐ Provide opportunities for students to clean and organize their supply boxes.
- ☐ Enlist student helpers to monitor the floor area around the lockers.

Sink/Counter Area

- ☐ Evaluate the usefulness of the organizational structures you have in place. Do the items on your counter have a function and a purpose, or is the counter becoming a clutter magnet?
- ☐ Use counter space to your advantage. Think about things you struggle to fit on your shelves, and see if you can store these more efficiently on your countertops.

Games/Recess Materials

- ☐ Buy games at garage or yard sales to replenish your game shelves for the fall.
- ☐ Enlist student assistance with organizing the game area.
- ☐ Insist that students be responsible for properly putting away the materials.
- ☐ Use organizational tools such as baggies and sturdy, plastic game boxes to keep things organized.
- ☐ Once a year, determine if games are still used. Ask students if they enjoy the games. Donate any that are outdated or not used often.
- ☐ Clean out your game area at least twice a year.

6: Keeping a Teacher Reference Binder

"For every minute
spent in organizing,
an hour is earned."
— Unknown

Wouldn't it be great to have an organized, central location to hold your school calendars, important memos, parent contact information, school and district policies, and curriculum and standards information, as well as special area and duty schedules? There are many different names for this helpful tool, such as "teacher binder," "desk binder," or "reference binder."

The idea of a teacher reference binder is not new. In fact, many teachers have created a general holding place for important documents. Consider the reasons to keep a teacher reference binder. One main reason is the large number of important documents teachers must manage on a daily basis. You need a holding place for these papers and documents. Rather than tossing important school schedules, calendars, or paperwork into a file folder or randomly placing them in a file cabinet, you can create one central, organized place for these papers. That way, you can locate them at a moment's notice, which promotes a much-needed sense of order in your daily routine.

> Rather than tossing important school schedules, calendars, or paperwork into a file folder or randomly placing them in a file cabinet, you can create one central, organized place for these papers. That way, you can locate them at a moment's notice, which promotes a much-needed sense of order in your daily routine.

TIPS FOR CHOOSING YOUR TEACHER REFERENCE BINDER

As you select a format for your teacher reference binder, consider the following characteristics:

Size

You can use any size you like for your teacher reference binder. It is a personal choice. Determine whether you want to contain large numbers of documents or just a few key items within your binder. This decision will guide you in choosing an appropriately sized binder. I usually use a 2-inch (5cm) binder to hold important paperwork. This way, as the year progresses, I know I can add more papers to my reference binder as needed without worrying that I'll run out of space.

Material

There are many different types of binders. Some teachers may want to use regular plastic three-ring binders. A couple of years ago, I found a great oversized leather binder at a local retail store. It is sturdy and durable, and will last a long time. The size and material also make it easy to locate at a moment's notice because it is different from other binders in my classroom.

Style

Choose a binder you like. You may want to choose a unique binder—one with a distinctive color, pattern, or material—so you can easily recognize and locate it when you need it.

Don't deliberate too much on the size, style, or material of your binder. Simply decide on something that appeals to you and then use it. You can always change it in the future to better suit your preferences.

Don't deliberate too much on the size, style, or material of your binder. Simply decide on something that appeals to you and then use it. You can always change it in the future to better suit your preferences.

WHAT DO I KEEP IN MY TEACHER REFERENCE BINDER?

What to include in your teacher reference binder is largely up to you. Some teachers like to include only the bare necessities in order to keep their binder trim and tidy. If this is your preference, you might only include items such as class lists, seating charts, weekly lesson plans, student medical concerns, and duty schedules. I personally like to include a wide range of papers and documents so most of my important papers are in one place; therefore, my binder is quite large.

I'll take you through a tour of my teacher reference binder to give you an idea of the kinds of things you might consider including in your binder. The papers and documents you include in your own binder will vary depending on your grade level and what you teach. I suggest using tabbed sections in order to keep papers grouped by like categories and to keep papers well ordered. Each of the following sections are separate tabs within my binder.

What to include in your teacher reference binder is largely up to you. Some teachers like to include only the bare necessities in order to keep their binder trim and tidy. If this is your preference, you might only include items such as class lists, seating charts, weekly lesson plans, student medical concerns, and duty schedules.

Class Lists and Parent Contact Information

In the first section of my teacher binder, I include a copy of my class lists (and any accompanying seating charts) as well as parent contact information (such as parent phone numbers, e-mail addresses, and any special information provided by parents). I teach more than one class of students, as many other teachers do, so it's important for me to have a current copy of each class list and any corresponding parent information so I can use it for a variety of purposes. I have a spreadsheet for each class that I use to check off homework and keep track of students' paperwork throughout the year. Sometimes I also use these class list spreadsheets to keep brief anecdotal notes about reading groups, or to document comments about behaviors, or even to make notations about parent communication throughout the year.

Emergency Building Information/Policies

You need to have all building and safety information close at hand in the event of an emergency. One of the first pieces of information I keep in this tabbed section is my school's building safety plan. It outlines procedures for fire, tornado, and lock-down situations. Be sure to include a copy of this information in your substitute teacher folder as well.

> Be sure to include a copy of your school's emergency policies in your substitute teacher folder.

Fire drill class lists: My school's secretaries type up fire drill class lists, and I keep my copies in this section. Keep copies of all classes that you teach in this section (not just your homeroom class if you teach more than one group of students) so you can pull whichever class list you need from this binder. I also keep copies of the class lists clipped to a magnet near the classroom door so I can quickly "grab and go" as needed for fire drills.

Tornado drill information: My school uses a tornado drill assigned areas sheet to provide details about where each class should go in the event of a tornado drill or an actual tornado.

School handbook: I also place a copy of our elementary handbook in this section of the binder. This handbook outlines specific policies regarding school hours, information about lunch, dress code, attendance policies, student records, bus rules, and more. It's often handy for answering occasional questions or situations that may arise through the school year.

Calendars and Schedules

In this section of the reference binder, I place copies of relevant calendars and schedules. There are many things to keep track of, and being current with specific dates of events is a key to staying organized for the school year.

School year calendar: The first document in this section is a current school year calendar. It is created by the school district, and it lists important dates, such as holidays, days off, winter and spring breaks, end-of-grading period dates, etc. Another calendar lists all of the months with those days marked on it. These two calendars go in the front of the binder because I access them frequently.

Monthly calendar: Next I include a blank printout of each individual month for the school year. This is especially helpful for building-specific dates, events, or activities within my own grade level. When my team meets for a grade-level meeting, it's great to have blank calendars handy so we can all jot down dates and events. This type of calendar is also useful for long-range planning through the school year (or you could print another set of monthly calendars for this purpose).

Schedules: Next I include various calendars, such as a special area schedule (art, music, physical education, library), a lunch/recess/bus duty schedule, and specialist schedules (including special education, speech, aide schedules). I've also included a calendar of days and times for our student safety patrols in this section to help

Tabs for Teacher Reference Binder

- Class Lists and Parent Contact Information
- Emergency Building Information/Policies
- Calendars and Schedules
- Important Memos
- Curriculum and Standards
- Progress Report/Grade Card Information
- Technology Tips Sheets

me keep track of students' assigned weeks. These are all important to have on hand so I can stay aware of assigned duties as well as be aware of the locations of different staff members in the event that I need to communicate with them throughout the school day.

Program schedules: Finally, I include a schedule printout for special programs such as DARE (Drug Abuse Resistance Education) and guidance classes. Having these schedules on hand helps me keep track of the time period and days remaining for these types of classes.

My school participates in a breakfast club, where staff members bring in breakfast items twice per year. This calendar reminds me when my breakfast duty is coming up.

Important Memos

This section is for important memos. These memos can range from information sheets from the school nurse to lists of students participating in various classes or clubs. You can break this section into more specialized tabs if you want. I've found that simply having a "Memos" tab in my reference binder works fine for me. Your memos will vary in nature from those listed here, depending on your grade level or subject area, as well as what paperwork your building provides to you, but these examples will give you an idea of the types of forms to include in this section.

> You can narrow down the memos category into more specialized tabs if you want.

Medical concerns: I include a medical concerns list and other related medical forms as the first items in the memos section of the binder. This list shows information that teachers need to know about students so we are aware of any student allergies or other conditions. You can use the blank Important Student Medical Information template on page 209 in the appendix to record important information regarding student allergies or other conditions.

Learning needs: Next in this section, I include any general paperwork regarding information related to students' learning needs. Although I do not keep IEPs (Individual Education Plans) in this section due to aspects of confidentiality (as well as the sheer thickness of these documents), I do keep general progress notes from previous teachers or informal notes about individual strengths or areas for improvement. This way, I have a bit of information about my students' needs before the school year starts, and I can begin to make decisions about differentiating instruction for students.

I also include information from our gifted teacher. I include a list of participants in our gifted program, as well as any sheets about program qualifications.

Policies and procedures: Also included in this section is an important document outlining our principal's general expectations for a variety of procedures. This packet includes information about expectations for arrival and dismissal, as well as general guidelines for hallway, lunchroom, playground, and assembly behavior.

I've included a packet detailing playground guidelines. My school's physical education teacher provides this helpful printout as a resource to help teachers and students understand expectations and basic rules for playground areas in order to promote safety during recess times.

Student supply list: I like to keep a copy of my grade-level school supply list in the memo section. A copy of this list comes in handy if I get a new student or if I simply want to send out a supply reminder to parents midyear for replenishing any school supplies that are running low.

Curriculum and Standards

The next section of the teacher reference binder deals with various aspects of the curriculum. Often my school district provides teachers with various guidelines and pacing guides that are important to have on hand as I plan my units. Having these documents in one place ensures that my weekly planning will go more smoothly. I can refer to these documents easily, which facilitates my lesson planning process.

Pacing guides: One of the first items in this section includes the district pacing guides for different subject areas. I reference these pacing guides weekly, so they need to be at the front of this section.

Subject-specific guidelines: Sometimes my school district provides various reference sheets related to different subject areas. For instance, we have an informative document describing how to perform our specific literacy assessments each year. It provides detailed information about timelines for giving our literacy assessments, as well as notes about how to fill out paperwork and folders related to the assessments.

Curriculum standards: I like to include copies of our grade-level curriculum standards in this section as well. Though it does add a bit of paperwork to the binder, I really like having this paperwork at my fingertips for planning purposes. I copy the standards on both sides in order to save paper, so it ends up not taking up too much space. Many teachers like this idea, but some would rather have a separate binder or reference book to consult for their particular curriculum standards or objectives in order to reduce the amount of paperwork in this section of their binder.

Progress Report/Grade Card Information

Progress reports or grade cards require remembering a lot of information, so I've found that it is a good idea to have a section in my teacher binder dealing with this topic. I can add important updates or step sheets to this section as needed.

I keep various information sheets regarding our reporting

process for grade cards in this section. Sometimes these are general information sheets, and sometimes they are specific to the electronic progress-reporting tool that we use in our district.

I keep a hard copy of the district grade card in this section in order to reference the various parts of the grade card that are included in this document.

Sometimes teachers receive information specific to reporting progress for students in special education programs (such as the speech program) or for English-language learners. I place these sheets in this tabbed section so I am aware of procedures for evaluating progress for these students.

Technology Tips Sheets

There is so much to learn each year with technology. Many times, my district provides professional development about a wide range of topics dealing with technology. Our building technology specialist is very adept in typing clear, concise step sheets or tip sheets that provide detailed information on specific programs or applications (such as the e-mail system, electronic attendance/lunch count procedures, online grade book information, and online substitute request program). These tip sheets come in handy when referencing programs over the course of the year.

> Keeping a teacher reference binder will provide you with much support throughout the course of your school year.

IN SUMMARY

Keeping a teacher reference binder will provide you with much support throughout the course of your school year. By containing important documents in one place, you can be assured that you will find any important piece of paper quickly and easily. Using this binder will help you plan more efficiently, and it will give you the ability to organize important paperwork that otherwise might be scattered throughout the classroom. Take some time to determine what items you want to incorporate into the binder, and start there. You can adjust and change the binder as needed.

Keep in mind also that it is important to clean out your binder annually so only current forms remain. With the potentially large number of sheets in this binder, you definitely do not want to allow for clutter to creep in. Keep it up to date to fully enjoy the benefits of your teacher reference binder.

Using this binder will help you plan more efficiently, and it will give you the ability to organize important paperwork that otherwise might be scattered.

Reference Binder Guidelines

- ☐ Choose a size, material, and style of binder that suits your purpose and preferences.

- ☐ Choose a size that will allow you to add papers throughout the school year.

- ☐ Choose a durable, sturdy binder.

- ☐ Determine helpful categories for tabs that suit your grade level and the subject areas you teach. Remember to group like documents together within tabs so it is easy to locate them.

- ☐ Keep your binder in a handy place so you can readily access it each day. If you choose to contain confidential information in your binder, be smart about placing it in a locked cabinet or drawer.

- ☐ At the end of the school year, clean out your binder so it contains only the most current forms. Remember to shred any personal information.

7: Conquering Paperwork and Filing

"The secret of getting ahead is getting started. The secret of getting started is breaking your complex, overwhelming tasks into small, manageable tasks, and then starting on the first one."

— Mark Twain

Teachers encounter a wide variety of paperwork: memos, student papers and files, parent notes, worksheets, papers to grade, and so much more. We have to be able to pick up a piece of paper and determine, within a matter of seconds, how to store, file, or use it.

An efficient paperwork system is a top priority for teachers. Digital and electronic technology has helped reduce the size of our paper files, but paperwork is still a very real part of our lives. An organized and consistent paperwork system is key to continued organizational success in the classroom. The system needs to accommodate each type of paperwork that you encounter. In this chapter, I'll provide suggestions for handling student and teacher files, worksheets, mail, and more. Being organized with your paperwork will go a long way in helping you to stay organized in nearly every other area of your classroom.

DEALING WITH INCOMING PAPERS

Numerous papers land on your desk and in your mailbox each day. When you handle paperwork—be it memos, notes, files, or student papers—I suggest you ask yourself as you touch every sheet of paper, "Do I even need this?"

Often, after retrieving my mail or when I begin to clean out a file, I will stand next to a trash can or recycle bin and toss things. Of course, I take time to carefully examine what is there so I am sure I am not getting rid of an important piece of mail. But this quick action feels great because I've immediately removed clutter and I know I'm keeping only the papers I need to reference in the future.

> An organized and consistent paperwork system is key to continued organizational success in the classroom.

When I receive a piece of mail at school, if it survives the plight of the trash can, it usually goes into my action file. Several times a week, I open my action file and determine what I need to do with the items inside. Mail can sometimes pile up because we have so much other paperwork. To avoid a pile, think about these questions when addressing mail:

- Will I need this piece of mail for a specific purpose? If so, file it in your action file.
- Will I need to sign something on this piece of mail and send it somewhere? If so, file it in your action file.
- Will I need to discuss this piece of mail with another teacher or colleague in the building? If so, place it in your action file.

If the piece of mail in question does not fit into these three categories, then it's likely you will not need it. If it's an advertisement, quickly decide whether you want to consider paying for the item, resource, or teacher conference. If not, recycle it now. You'll reduce the clutter in your mind and in your classroom!

THE "RIGHT" SYSTEM

Some teachers may feel that there is one "right" or correct way to deal with paperwork and files. Usually this is because they are thrilled with the results of the system they are using, and that's great. There are so many options when it comes to filing. There are various types of folders, prepackaged filing systems with ready-made labels, and systems with special color coding. But sometimes the sheer number of choices for filing is overwhelming and makes it difficult for many people to decide what to do.

Teachers sometimes fear that there really is one best way to conquer filing, and this just isn't so. It's important to determine what will work for you. In other words, you need to develop systems that you will use for the long haul. Factor in your style and color preferences, but first decide how you want to actually organize

Teachers sometimes fear that there really is one best way to conquer filing, and this just isn't so. It's important to determine what will work for you.

your files. If you want to change your filing system later on, you can. Make it work for you in the here and now.

TYPES OF FILE ORGANIZERS

One of the hardest decisions in dealing with paperwork is determining what kind of file system or organizer to use.

We often need to store some papers or documents on our desks for easy access and convenience. Many types of desktop file organizers are available. Some of the most important considerations include the space needed for files and personal preferences for the filing system you choose. If you need a good amount of space for files, or if you are unsure how large your file pile on your desk might grow in the course of a school year, it is a good idea to consider a stacking set of horizontal file holders. These look like small shelves that are a little larger than an 8½" × 11" (22cm × 28cm) piece of paper and just a few inches deep. These file holders come in various colors and materials, from plastic to metal. Using horizontal file holders is helpful because they contain the files while keeping them accessible. You can always add another holder to your set as your files grow. Remember not to store too many papers on your desk though.

Another possible filing method is to use a vertical filing system. These systems range from slots that hold the files upright to angled wire holders. The downside to a vertical file system is that you are a bit more limited in terms of space because fewer files can squeeze in between each section, and you cannot add additional sections to this file system.

Another unique idea for storing files on your teacher desk is to use magazine file boxes. This is a creative way to contain a number of manila files, providing relatively easy access to your paperwork.

PAPERWORK FILES

After you've decided on which type of file organizer will work best for you, you'll need to determine exactly what files you need to file within your organizer. Although your files may vary depending on the grade level or subject you teach, here are some common categories.

Action File

Teachers have many tasks to attend to in the course of the day, so an action file is critical. Some teachers may not want to use an action file because they've found it becomes a catchall for miscellaneous papers. However, the kind of action file I recommend is one that contains only papers that require you to take action, such as signing off on a parent-teacher communication, completing staff release forms, placing book orders, or attending to other office paperwork.

Other teachers may shy away from such a file because they are afraid that if something is inside a file folder, they will forget about it. This is where some change in habits may need to take place. If you have a central location for things you need to read, respond to, or sign, you will soon see the benefits of having this organized system. Sometimes if I am afraid that I'll forget to actively use my action file, I will place any important paperwork directly on my desk so I know I need to take action on it the next day.

To "File" File

During the course of a school day, we take out papers from files, binders, and curriculum books. At the end of the day, we end up with a stack of papers that need to be filed properly, or we accumulate a lot more paper clutter. There are many ways to deal with this daily filing concern. One way to deal with it is to file papers daily. This sounds easy, but with time constraints and interruptions, it isn't always easy to find time. Still, many teachers truly prefer that whenever they take papers out of their files, binders, or other holding places to teach lessons, they file those loose pages back into the correct spot that very same day. If you can do this on a regular basis, I think that is a great goal. But for some teachers (including myself), it's just not possible to keep on top of papers as consistently. So for this reason, I established a file for myself called To File. This file label is not unique, because many teachers have such a file pile. But to discourage true clutter from creeping up, I decided that I needed a limit for myself, and a visual limit was more conducive for me than a weekly goal for filing. So I created the one-inch rule. This means that at no time can I allow my file pile to get any thicker than 1 inch (3cm). It is a manageable task for me, and it gives me permission to have a bit of a pile just sitting there waiting for me to file. It takes the pressure off, if you will, because I know that I will be attending to the pile at a later (set) time.

> The one-inch filing rule means at no time can I allow my file pile to get any thicker than 1 inch (3cm) ... It gives me permission to have a bit of a pile just sitting there waiting for me to file.

To Grade File

Although I try to grade papers at home after work, it is not always possible. So I like to keep papers in a location that is easily accessible. I can pull papers from my To Grade file during my planning period or when I have a few extra minutes. It's a nice way to keep papers organized and in one spot.

Memos File

Keeping track of memos can be a bit daunting. I like to keep a file just for memos. I can keep track of important information and know at all times where this information can be found. I try to clean out the Memos file several times a year so it does not become too large or filled with outdated information.

To Copy File

It's a good idea to have a separate file box or pile for copying. If you have parent volunteers, you can work with them to set up a central location where they can always determine, at a moment's notice, where to pick up any worksheets or papers that need to be copied. It's handy to have a To Copy file so you can put worksheets there when you are planning for the week ahead or as you do some future planning. You may not need the copies right away, but you will have them copied, and therefore, be more prepared for units to come.

STORING WORKSHEETS

You can be prepared for daily lessons by creating storage for your curriculum worksheets. An organized, well-ordered storage system allows you to easily pull what you need for your daily instruction. There are a variety of ways to store worksheets.

Use a Mailbox Sorter

One of the best organizational tools in any classroom is a mailbox sorter system. You may already use this type of system because it is useful for organizing a variety of materials. I have two of these sorters in my classroom. I use one of them for a student mailbox system (more on how to organize student mail in Chapter 13). I use the other sorter for all of the copied worksheets I need for instruction.

I highly recommend you invest in a mailbox sorter, no matter the subject or grade level you teach. Space is precious, and all of those worksheets must live somewhere!

An important part of using this tool is to decide how you want to organize your worksheets. Do you want to organize by subject area or perhaps by days of the week, or just as needed? It's logical for most elementary teachers to organize by subject because they often have multiple subjects to teach. Middle and high school teachers may have more flexibility in organizing their worksheets. They might organize by unit or by the week, placing all worksheets for a current week in one section.

My sorter has four columns (or sections), and I found that sectioning it off by subject works well for me. Using a worksheet/mailbox sorter system allows you to quickly and easily find whatever worksheets you need.

When you pull worksheets into a file sorter ahead of time, you already have what you need for the coming week. You won't need to search for the worksheets you need each day.

Use a Weekly File Sorter

In addition to a mailbox sorter, many teachers benefit from using a weekly file sorter where you can store all worksheets you'll need for the week ahead. It may seem a bit redundant to house the majority of your worksheets in a larger sorter and then put worksheets for the week ahead in a separate sorter, but when you pull worksheets into this smaller sorter ahead of time, you already have what you need for the coming week. You won't need to search for the worksheets you need each day because they'll already be in your weekly sorter. Using a weekly file sorter provides structure for the week ahead. This is a personal choice and preference. You may want to modify or change this idea to fit your personality. It's just one way to think about organizing your materials.

The weekly file sorter is much smaller than a mailbox sorter. It usually can rest on your teacher desk or on a table or shelf. The weekly file sorter can be a metal vertical file with file folders labeled by days of the week, or simply a wire or plastic set of file holders stacked upon one another, each file slot standing for one day of the week. This is a great way for teachers to ensure that their weekly paperwork is at their fingertips and ready to go for daily instruction. Using this tool gives you a great feeling, knowing that you are well prepared for the week ahead. Gathering the worksheets together for the next day is an easy process when you use a weekly file sorter.

Managing Extra Copies

Most teachers find it necessary to make a few extra copies of worksheets and keep them on hand for absent students or for students who lose worksheets or assignments. But how do you efficiently store these papers? There are a variety of ways to store loose papers, and here are three ways I have found to be effective:

Use a crate and hanging files. A crate works well for holding extra worksheets. Students can access it easily. To use a crate for this purpose, designate a hanging file for each subject area you teach. When passing out papers during lessons, assign a student to place additional copies in the extra file for the subject area you are addressing at that time.

Use a file sorter or stacked trays. Another idea for storing extra copies is to use a file sorter (or magazine rack) to neatly contain extra worksheets. The one drawback to this option is cost. Some teachers also find that it works fine to use simple file folders for each subject in stacked trays placed in a central location.

Maintain a simple pile. In a pinch, I've kept a running pile of extra worksheets on top of a file cabinet (there's really no order to it, but because I go through and recycle the pages often enough, I can essentially grab whatever my students need quickly and efficiently). Instead of students maintaining these papers, I keep them handy, and students know to ask me when they need another worksheet. Although this creates a bit more work for me, using this system allows me to easily keep track of students who tend to lose papers. I can use this information to help them by talking to them about organizing their materials more efficiently the next time around.

Store documents electronically. When possible, create opportunities for storing documents electronically. You can include copies of frequently used documents on either a class website or a blog. This type of storage allows parents to access the worksheets at any time (which helps with fewer trips back to school to get missing assignments). Posting worksheets electronically is an especially helpful practice for various documents that students will use often throughout the year, such as reading response forms, word study activity sheets, or other curricular worksheets. Another option is to simply send parents e-mail attachments of specific worksheets as you are working with students on a particular unit. This way, you are not only providing extra copies for students should they need them, but you are also giving parents timely information about what students are studying in class.

There are many more options for storing those extra worksheets, but the main thing to keep in mind when storing any additional worksheets is to clean out your storage system every two or three weeks. If you keep a master copy of the worksheet, you can recycle extras after this time period or after the assignment due date. Otherwise, your extras files will become messy and cluttered. You can ask students to help you with this task.

STUDENT FILES

Most teachers realize the importance of keeping student files to store important documentation and information as the year progresses. Elementary, middle, and high school teachers can benefit from creating organized student files to keep good records, keep track of parent communication, and determine students' strengths and areas for improvement as the school year progresses. A traditional filing cabinet is a great place to keep your student files because it provides more privacy for confidential information and you'll have plenty of room to add to the files. There is no set rule about what kinds of things to keep or store in these files, but it's a good idea to consider keeping the following items within your student files.

Student Surveys and Inventories

I use a variety of student surveys or inventories to track, monitor, and guide instruction for my students. I often place these surveys in the front of my student files so I can access them quickly when I need to look at student preferences, interests, or learning styles. Keeping these surveys handy can help you remain aware of your students' needs through the school year. You might use an inventory to gain specific information about students' background knowledge, preferences, strengths, or weaknesses in a particular subject area. You also might ask students to fill out a general interest inventory to get to know them better as individuals, especially at the beginning of the year. I like to use a general interest inventory, but I also use a student survey to get a feel for how students are feeling about school after the first few weeks. I've found that giving students a little time to adjust to routines and schedules helps them open up about themselves as learners later on. You can use the Student Inventory Sheet on page 210 in the appendix to gather important information about how your students are feeling about the start of the school year, their strengths, areas of concern, and any questions they have about classroom procedures.

Vital Documents

As a teacher, I need to keep track of student accommodations and modifications on a daily basis, so I keep a copy of student Individual Education Plans (IEPs) within my student files. It's very important to keep this information confidential, so keep your files in a secure place. In addition to IEP records, I store my conference records in my student files so I can access them quickly and easily.

Parent Communications

It's important to keep lines of communication open with parents. I like to store copies of e-mails and parent notes in student files. I have a good record of communication with parents. You can also keep a running record of communication with each of your parents by using the Parent Contact Form on page 211 in the appendix. This form is a quick and easy method for keeping track of how often you've communicated with parents. It allows you to easily determine which parents you may not have gotten in touch with for a period of time, so you can perhaps send them a quick communication about how their child is doing in school.

The Importance of Labeling

I would be remiss if I didn't mention the importance of labeling! As are most teachers, I am a big fan of labeling for several reasons. First of all, it gives a clean, crisp look to your files, containers, boxes, and bins. Labeling is helpful for students so that they can easily return books and materials by themselves after using them. (For primary teachers, it's often a good idea to include pictures along with the labels for students who may need support with reading.)

It is important to take some time to create labels in order to establish an atmosphere of organization. Doing so will promote a sense of order for the long haul. Students pick up on our systems for organizing, and many students love to help with labeling all around the room! Whether you use a labeler (which I highly recommend) or create labels by hand, you are establishing an efficient way to maintain your organizational systems.

Copies of Classroom Samples and Assessments

Some of the most important items to store in a student's file folder are classroom work samples and assessments. Make copies of various formative and summative assignments to collect a representative sample of student progress. This is especially important to have on hand for parent conferences, but it can also be an excellent resource for you in guiding your instructional decisions for students during the year. If an assignment seems to provide significant documentation about a student's performance, I make a copy of the assignment for my records. This can be time-consuming but well worth my time and effort because it informs my instruction and gives me an opportunity to refer back to the students' strengths and areas for improvement.

CREATE TIME FOR FILING

It is important to find time for the process of filing. Because I keep a one-inch rule, I need to be sure to schedule time to file papers, or the one-inch rule will turn into a two-, three-, or four-inch rule! Papers can build up quickly in your classroom, so it's critical to build time into your weekly schedule for filing, whether it's once a week during a planning period, or before or after school. If you file on a regular basis, you'll know exactly where all of your paperwork is, and you can put your papers away in a matter of minutes instead of hours. Filing is often a laborious, tedious process, but once completed, I feel so much more on track, organized, and ready to face the next day.

> Papers can build up quickly in your classroom, so it's critical to build time into your weekly schedule for filing, whether it's once a week during a planning period or before or after school.

Filing Do's and Don'ts

Do's

- [ ] Give careful consideration to your filing system setup. Consider color, style, and type of files you want to use.

- [ ] Use a filing system that you think will work well for your natural tendencies. If you are a piler, use stackable trays; if you like to see every folder, use vertical file holders.

- [ ] Label your files neatly and carefully.

- [ ] Keep confidential records safe and out of sight.

- [ ] Create time to file your papers. Assign a day or time during the week, or use a visual reminder, such as a one-inch rule to help you keep up with this task.

- [ ] Purge files at least once a school year so that you have room for new papers.

Don'ts

- [ ] Don't worry too much about whether you are "doing it right." Remember that there is really no right or wrong way to establish a filing system, unless you have none at all!

- [ ] Don't create too many desk files. Doing so will promote clutter on your desk area. Only create desk files for those items you need to access on a fairly regular basis.

- [ ] Don't use filing cabinets for miscellaneous storage. You need the filing cabinet space for files! Consider other storage options for materials and supplies.

8: Organizing Curriculum Materials

"Each problem that I solved became a rule which served afterwards to solve other problems."

— René Descartes

From teacher manuals to resource books, idea files, loose worksheets, printables from the Internet, and more, teachers have scores of curriculum materials to keep organized. It is vital that you develop and maintain a system for storing your curriculum materials. There are several things to keep in mind when storing these resources. First, be sure to have ample storage space. Dedicate at least one, if not two, shelving units for your books, resources, and teacher binders. Second, you need to determine how you want to store your resources on these shelves. Third, it's important to be open to changing your system as needed because your needs and preferences may change. In this chapter, I'll share various ways to store your teacher resource books and help you determine ways to effectively maintain your system.

THE BINDER SYSTEM

Ever since I started teaching, I've loved using three-ring binders to contain various worksheets, documents, and curriculum papers. It's great to see the binders neatly stacked, labeled, and ready for me to access at a moment's notice. The idea of utilizing binders to store loose pages is certainly nothing new, but developing and maintaining an organized, sensible system using binders can help to facilitate your teaching resources in many ways.

Shortly after I began teaching, I happened upon the idea of using plastic sleeves within my binders to further organize papers. Although I certainly didn't invent the idea, it became almost an obsession of mine. Though somewhat costly, I saw the benefits of using these plastic sleeves, which include:

- preventing pages from ripping out of my binders
- prolonging the life of the pages by keeping them clean and free of wrinkles and tears
- making it easier to organize papers in distinct categories within the binders

I grouped the papers by subject, topic, or unit.

TYPES OF BINDERS

Using binders to organize curricular worksheets, idea pages, or documents can facilitate your instruction and help you become a more organized teacher.

Content Area/Unit Binders

As you consider using binders to organize your curriculum papers, first determine for which subjects, topics, or units you need binders. For instance, one of the subjects I teach is reading, so I have many binders devoted to various aspects of reading.

Some of my binders include topics related to methods of instruction. Here are some examples of the various reading binders I keep:

- Guided Reading
- Literature Circles
- Reading Mini Lessons
- Independent Reading
- Shared Reading/Read Aloud

I have other binders devoted to specific novels we might use for shared reading during the school year. Still other reading binders contain miscellaneous ideas or worksheets that I find interesting. These I might label "Reading Ideas."

In addition to reading, I teach writing and spelling. Each subject has its own set of binders, including unit binders and binders for mini lessons, worksheets, activities, and games.

Your specific binders will be based on what subject(s) you teach and may vary significantly. These lists will give you an idea of how I've organized my curriculum papers based on what I currently teach.

Idea File Binders

A second type of binder I like to use is an Idea File Binder. Through the years, and especially at the beginning of my teaching career, I

Using binders to organize curricular worksheets, idea pages, or documents can facilitate your instruction and help you become a more organized teacher.

couldn't get my hands on enough idea books. I wanted to gather as much information as I could about setting up classrooms, classroom management, tips for motivating students, and so on. The idea pages I gleaned from these books didn't always fit cleanly into specific subject areas, but I knew that I needed to organize these pages so I could access them quickly. I labeled them Idea File Binders. Some examples of these types of binders include:

- Parent/Teacher Conferences
- Classroom Management/Discipline
- Organizing the Classroom

Decide what topics you want to learn more about, or what tips you want to keep handy, and begin collecting and storing those helpful articles or worksheets related to these topics in binders. One important tip: Don't save an article or worksheet simply for the sake of saving it. Be sure that what you are saving has real value for you. If you believe you will truly use a specific idea, tip, or activity in your classroom, then it should go into your binder. But be choosy, because if you add too many pages to your Idea File Binders, you will promote lots of clutter in your classroom!

Seasonal/Holiday Binders

I also use Seasonal/Holiday Binders. I have four of these binders in which I've collected various activities, worksheets, and pages that relate to different holidays. I use some of these pages throughout the school year, and having them in a specific place keeps me from scrounging around for the materials in the depths of my file cabinets when I need them! I usually contain two to three months within each binder. I have a September/October binder, a November/December binder, a binder for January through March, and a binder for April through the end of the school year.

Don't save an article or worksheet simply for the sake of saving it. Be sure that what you are saving has real value for you.

Usually, it's necessary to have at least 1½ inch (4cm) or 2-inch (5cm) binders, because I often store lots of different worksheets in them. Using 3-inch (8cm) binders can help you contain lots of papers, but they are sometimes a bit unwieldy and heavy, so you will need to decide which sizes work best for your needs.

MAINTAINING THE BINDER SYSTEM

Binders are such helpful tools when it comes to organizing a great deal of paperwork. Binders do take up space, but they allow for portability. You can just grab a binder and take out what you need to use or copy for your class. Binders are neat and durable, but to keep them useful, it's important to keep several things in mind.

Importance of Regular Filing

To maintain your binder system, regularly file curriculum papers back into your binders. There are many ways to do this. One way is to use the "1-inch rule" described in Chapter 7. Using a system like this helps keep you on track because it is a tangible visual aid so you know when you must begin to file in order to prevent a back-up of papers. I've had a couple of school years where I just couldn't get to my filing as regularly as I wanted to, and I had to sit with all of those papers during the summer and file for such a length of time. It was painful! I learned after those experiences that I needed to find a method by which I could easily manage filing my paperwork on a more regular basis. The "1-inch rule" is just one method for managing your filing process.

Some teachers want to return their curriculum papers to binders right away, and they file all of their papers daily, which eliminates large piles of papers to file in the future.

Another idea is to file them after completing a study unit. You might pull various pages for instruction, and then put them in a tray or folder and file them after your unit is complete. Choose whatever system of filing will work best for you.

Purging Files in the Binders

To keep your "binder system" neat and orderly, you must take the time to purge your files (yes, there's the "purge" word again). Go through and determine how useful your curricular worksheets are from time to time. There is no point in keeping old, outdated, or multiple copies of the same worksheets. I recommend purging your binders at least once every year. You might decide to purge a few of your binders each month so you do not feel overwhelmed by the process. One helpful tip is to periodically take home a binder and purge it in the comfort of your home. I do this from time to time. This way, I'm not spending additional time at school, but I can still complete this important task.

> There is no point in keeping old, outdated, or multiple copies of the same worksheets. I recommend purging your binders at least once every year.

Find ways to purge that will work for you. If you don't take time to occasionally purge your binders, you will become a binder pack rat, and you will have scores of binders in your room (which adds up to clutter!). Multiple binders in the same category add to the amount of material you need to look through to find what you are really after. If you feel hesitant about purging your binders, review the tips in Chapter 3 about the benefits of purging. As a side benefit of purging my binders, I've found worksheets or activities that I had forgotten about. Purging refreshes my memory about some curricular activities I may want to use in my instruction during the year.

TEACHER MANUALS AND RESOURCE BOOKS

How do we store the multitude of teacher manuals, resource guides, and idea books that we have? These materials are a critical part of our daily routine, so we need to find ways to effectively store them. In storing these resources, you need to consider three things:

1. **Convenience:** However you store your teacher resources, you need to be able to access them with ease on a daily basis. Can you grab what you need at any point in the school day? Are your resources easy to retrieve and put back? Or do you have to walk to a far corner of your room for a teacher manual or a textbook?
2. **Efficiency:** Evaluate how long it takes you to access your resources and return them after use. Find a system that lets you do this as quickly and easily as possible.
3. **Location:** Determine the best place to store your materials in order to carry out instruction in the best manner possible.

Storage Options for Resource Books, Idea Books, and Manuals

Shelf Resource Books by Subject Area. One way to store your teacher resources and manuals is to designate a shelf (or a portion of a shelf) for a specific content area. For instance, if you are a self-contained elementary teacher, you might label a shelf for each of the subjects you teach. You can label a shelf for word study/spelling, another shelf for reading, one for writing, and others for math, social studies, and science.

If you are an upper elementary, middle school, or high school teacher with a departmental model for instruction, you might be able to organize your resources more specifically. You can designate certain shelves for your units, or you can organize with a timeline in mind. Specifically, you can place the resources you primarily use in the fall on the left side of the shelf, and then progress to adding other resources that you use later in the year on the right side. This approach follows the model of how we read from left to right.

I recommend that you organize by subject. Placing your resource books, idea books, and manuals haphazardly on shelving units will cause a great deal of frustration during your daily instruction, especially if you have a large number of resources. If you do not create a structure for organizing your resources, you won't be able to find what you need. You will feel so much happier when your resources are arranged in a neat, structured manner. You will know where to find the resources you need, right when you need them!

Use Bins or Tubs. Another way to contain your resources and manuals is to designate bins or tubs for them. I've tried this method in the past and have found it helpful. In using tubs or bins, I sorted my teacher idea books by subject. Then I estimated how many bins I might need before I bought them. I also labeled them by subject so I could easily locate the resources I needed during the day. Using tubs and bins takes up a fair amount of space (as opposed to just placing books on a shelf by subject). In addition, the tubs or bins can get heavy, so you need to be careful when taking them on and off of shelves.

Use the File Cabinet. Many teachers like to store teacher resource books in their file cabinets. If you choose to do this, I recommend storing them spine up, so you can easily identify the title of the resource book you need. In addition, if you have a lot of books for a certain subject, you can devote an entire drawer to a subject area. Using a file cabinet in this manner can make retrieving resources an easy task. On the flip side, it takes up a lot of space that you could otherwise use for important files.

> Think carefully about how you want to store your teaching resources. Your manuals, resources and idea books are important parts to planning your yearly curriculum, so you want them to be easily accessible and organized.

Often-Used Resource Books

When you use some of the same resources each day, it's a good idea to pull them together (even if they differ by subject area) and contain them in a central location. That way, you can just grab them when you need them for daily lessons. One way to do this is to use a desktop divider organizer. I purchased a sturdy metal divider that has wider spaces in between so I can place textbooks or thicker resource books in it. I like to place the divider organizer on the table next to my overhead projector. That way I can refer to any of my often-used resources quickly and efficiently. You don't have to use an organizer to store these items; you can simply place them neatly on a small table or desk in a central location. I find, however, that having the metal organizer keeps things crisp and ordered.

Managing Resources

- ☐ As you decide how to store your curriculum materials, keep these tips in mind so you can find what you need when you need it.

- ☐ Decide how you want to organize your resources (by subject, unit of study, or chronologically by teaching timeline).

- ☐ Decide if you want to place resources on shelves or use bins, tubs or filing cabinets.

- ☐ Consider housing a few select resources or manuals in a central location in your room (such as on a small table near the overhead projector). These resources should be ones you access nearly every day.

- ☐ Purge your binders and resource materials at least once per year. See Chapter 3 for more ideas on purging and how to ROLL with your clutter.

- ☐ Be open to trying different systems for storing your teacher resources and manuals. There is no one right way to organize your resources. Just try a system for organizing, and be willing to make a change later on if you don't like it.

9: Lesson Planning

"He who fails to plan,
plans to fail."

— Unknown

As a teacher, you must be able to effectively plan instruction that is based on your district's curriculum standards. You also need to initiate lessons that are engaging, specific, and relevant to your students. You need to begin lessons with a sense of energy and enthusiasm, and you also need to have sufficient materials and supplies with which to teach. So what is the essential ingredient for making all that happen? The essential ingredient for effective lesson planning isn't the latest and greatest software, the most impressive plan book, or even a neat, tidy format. The most important element for effective lesson plans is time. Sounds so simple, doesn't it? Over the years, my experience has taught me that time is the "it" that allows me to develop a careful and proper lesson plan. Of course, many other elements help with lesson planning (more on this soon), but giving yourself the gift of time will promote a higher standard for your teaching and a better outcome for your classroom instruction.

CARVE OUT STRUCTURED TIME

As teachers, we hardly have a spare moment during a given day. Almost every minute is tied to working with students, fulfilling a duty, attending a building meeting, copying, filing, e-mailing, or talking with another teacher or staff member about a student, lesson idea, or schedule item. So how can teachers find time during the course of a day to work on lesson plans? The only way I've ever found time to plan for lessons in the way I truly desire is to carve out time. I used to scramble to complete a week's worth of lesson plans at the end of the day on a Friday, and by then, I would be so mentally exhausted that I could barely focus or concentrate on the task at hand. I wanted

Focusing on one subject at a time allowed me to lesson plan in smaller chunks of time and use my planning period or time before or after school more effectively.

desperately to feel that I was prepared for the week ahead, so I desired to complete my plans on the preceding Friday. But in so doing, I was compromising myself because my lesson plans, while generally sound, lacked some essential elements, like a creative aspect to my mini lessons or a list of important things to copy (or to do) prior to the week ahead. On Monday morning, I would need to further tweak my plans to feel truly prepared for the week ahead. I knew that I couldn't shortchange my students or myself, so I was only creating more work for myself. I knew then that I needed to either plan for more time or change the where and when of lesson planning so I was more refreshed and able to concentrate. I decided to break up my lesson planning and focus on one subject at a time. This allowed me to plan in smaller chunks of time, and I could use my planning period or time before or after school (when it is quiet in the room) more effectively. I can focus much more clearly on my lesson plans during these calmer periods of the day.

Don't limit yourself to planning periods and time before and after school. Perhaps you can find little "pockets" of time during which to plan. Would any of these options work for you?

- **Student study period.** Some teachers work on aspects of lesson plans during the last twenty minutes of the day when their students have a study period. Students generally need to remain quiet to do some studying, so you might be able to capitalize on this time for yourself.
- **Supplemental lesson time.** If another teacher (such as a guidance teacher, a DARE officer, or a technology teacher) comes to your room to teach a supplementary lesson, you may be able to work on lesson plans while he or she carries out instruction for the class.

- **Lunch hour.** Lesson planning during lunch isn't necessarily a desirable option. I don't enjoy working on lesson plans during this time because I like to take a break, but often the material is fresher in my mind during this time of day so it is easier to be creative. Planning during my lunch break does provide me with another option when time is of the essence.

- **Create time in your lesson plans.** It may be helpful to look carefully at your current lesson plans to see where you can carve out some time for lesson planning. Look at your current class periods to evaluate the times that you teach. Aside from the times I've already mentioned, is there a small block of ten or fifteen minutes you could use to work on planning a subject area for the following week? Perhaps your students have a warm-up activity that they do before a class. If that activity doesn't require much teacher assistance, you could work on filling in some plans for a subject on your lesson plans. Or maybe you initiate a special reward where your students can earn an extra recess, game, or other privilege at the end of the week or month. Though these moments are few and far between, if it is possible during those instances to work on lesson plans, I suggest you capitalize on them so you take advantage of every small bit of time.

FOCUS ON ONE SUBJECT OR CLASS AT A TIME

Where you plan your lessons—whether at school, at home, or elsewhere—depends on many factors, including family commitments and other responsibilities. I was able to do my lesson planning during school hours, but I realized that I needed to plan my week ahead in chunks. That means that I would take my time and plan each subject, one at a time, during a few planning periods or before or after school toward the end of the week. That way, I could focus on developing carefully crafted plans for each subject area without rushing. My vision for trying to finish all of my lesson plans in one sitting quickly became a thing of the past, and now I feel much better planning in this fashion.

For example, on a Thursday I would map out plans for my math class for the week ahead. I would take the teacher's manual and my curriculum standards, and sit and think carefully about what we covered as a class this week. I would reflect on whether some re-teaching or enrichment lessons were needed and determine what else I needed to teach within the current unit. I could dialogue with myself more smoothly using this method, and my thoughts weren't rushing to other subjects that I still needed to plan. This singular

Prioritize Your Time for Lesson Planning

Although teachers often do not have a great deal of free time, we sometimes need to evaluate whether we are using time wisely in the first place. Think about the tasks you perform on a daily basis. Do you visit for long periods of time with colleagues before or after school? Do you spend lots of time at the copy machine, copying pages for several units ahead of schedule? Do you spend time filing or tidying up? Each of these activities holds merit for various reasons. However, if you are finding that time for lesson planning is scarce, I suggest you think carefully about how you spend your time on a given day and determine whether there are any activities that you can cut short or perhaps do at a later time so that lesson plans become a higher priority. When teachers are committed to putting creative energy, effort, and time into developing their lesson plans, other things seem to fall into place. When your lesson plans are concise, creative, and well thought-out, you are well on your way toward efficiency and purpose for the long haul.

focus freed me to think about creative ways to build upon my instruction for each individual subject area. My mind wasn't distracted because my goal for planning was specific and targeted. Using this method for lesson planning helps me feel a bit more relaxed because while I'm planning one subject, I know I will make time later in the week to plan my other subjects.

HAVE MATERIALS HANDY

When you plan for the week ahead, don't forget to gather all of the resources and manuals you need to effectively plan for lessons. Whether the resource or manual is for the purpose of planning a mini lesson, the main ("practice") portion of a lesson, or for ideas on assessment, it's good practice to have things handy and at your fingertips. Ideally, you will have these resources near your teacher desk or wherever you work on your lesson plans. For some subjects, such as reading, I often have several idea books and resource guides crowding my space as I plan, but I find this effective because sometimes I'll need one resource for an idea for a mini lesson, while the bulk of my lesson may come from another guide. If you don't keep your resources and manuals nearby, you may find yourself wasting a lot of valuable planning time simply retrieving items. Taking time to gather your resources before sitting down to complete your lesson plans will help to promote a smooth work session, as well as a sense of efficiency.

CREATE A YEARLY PLAN

One of the best ways to prepare for an upcoming school year is to map out your curriculum for the year. Especially for a new teacher, but just as important for seasoned teachers, a yearly plan gives clear direction and perspective for the concepts, units, and objectives you need to teach. A yearly plan gives structure for lessons in the months ahead. When you consult your yearly plan as you create weekly lesson plans, you will quickly see what you still need to teach, whether you are on track, or whether you need to adjust your pace. A yearly plan can help you prioritize when so many other things attempt to crowd your already busy week's plans. You can certainly alter your yearly plan as things come up, but already having a basic layout for the structure of your units ensures that you are aware of your overall curriculum and your district expectations, standards, and routines. It may be helpful to work on your yearly plan with another teaching partner, especially if you teach the same subject areas. Working with another teacher promotes helpful feedback, and you may generate more ideas together than alone.

One of the best ways to prepare for an upcoming school year is to map out your curriculum for the year.

Be sure to gather all the materials that you will need to create your yearly plan. Here is a list of possible materials you may want to have on hand:

- District/state standards
- District pacing guides (pacing guides generally provide a framework by month or number of weeks to complete units of study)
- Textbooks you use for your units of study
- Teacher resource books/guides (these are books or guides that you have personally found useful for preparing various units of study)
- Previous year's lesson plans (I do not advocate incorporating the exact lesson plans from the previous year because students' needs vary so widely and curriculum requirements change frequently, but, for general references, it may be helpful to reference the previous year's lesson plans to get an idea of time frames for units)

You can use the Yearly Curriculum Map in the appendix to help you plan for your year ahead. There is a blank map for your use on page 212 and a completed example on page 214.

KNOW YOUR CURRICULUM

Knowing your curriculum may seem obvious—and even ingrained in our minds as teachers (because good practice indicates that most teachers are aware of curriculum expectations)—but sometimes, even the most conscious teachers can get sidetracked or distracted from the curriculum due to a number of factors (interruptions to daily schedules, assemblies, special holiday projects, and so on). Be sure to consult the standards for your curriculum each week as you are planning your lessons. Have these standards at hand as you are planning, whether you access them online, in a book format, or in your teacher reference binder. Although we should allow for creativity and individuality in lessons, we still must strive to maintain our curriculum and foster a strong sense of commitment to our district standards for instruction. Curriculum standards build upon one another from year to year, so by following curriculum standards carefully, we ensure that we are doing our part in the current year to continue our students' learning in a meaningful, logical path.

COMPONENTS OF A GOOD LESSON PLAN

There are many variations on what to include within your lesson plans. Some people are very detailed. If this is your style, you may want to bullet-point or number the steps of your lesson very specifically. Others prefer to be more fluid, in which case you would simply write down the general idea or title of a lesson plan and perhaps add one or two general lesson notes, such as a page reference or a notation to a specific activity page. There are, however, some specific things to keep in mind when considering elements of your lesson plan.

Include a List of Materials

No matter how detailed your lesson plan, you must keep track of what materials you need for your upcoming lessons. Allow enough space to indicate what materials you need. For instance, do you need copies of various worksheets? Be sure to write it down. Do you need to set up a lab for an experiment? What supplies or materials do you need for this purpose? Do you need to set up chart paper for recording class ideas for a lesson? If you jot this down in your plans, you will be more prepared for your lesson on the day you intend to teach it.

Provide Details About Lesson Procedures

In crafting my lesson plans, I like to provide a brief step-by-step procedure for my weekly lesson plans. Sometimes I use asterisks or a numbered list to write what exactly will take place in each lesson. I usually refer to specific pages in teacher manuals where necessary so I am organized and able to refer to various resources quickly and efficiently. I like to indicate what the lesson content includes, as well as the topic or unit number if the lessons are numbered within a teacher's manual. What you include in your lesson plans is, in large part, up to you. Some school districts require that teachers include very specific objectives or standards within their lesson plans. If so, keep in mind the space you may need to include such information in your lesson plans.

LESSON PLAN FORMAT

Now that you have an idea of what you need to include in your lesson plans and have a rough idea of how much room you'll need, you can find a lesson plan format that will work for you. There's a plethora of formats from which you can choose, and you can create a custom lesson plan format, whether from a lesson plan book, a computer-generated source, or another source. When it comes to selecting a lesson plan format, the most important thing to consider is your own personality. Do you like things to be exact with labels for each and every subject, class, or period? Or do you appreciate a more "open box" format, where you can write your plans

> When it comes to selecting a lesson plan format, the most important thing to consider is your own personality.

more generically? Your format also will depend, in part, on the grade level and subjects you teach. Following is an overview of each format.

Commercial Lesson Plan Book

Many teachers appreciate the layout of commercial lesson plan books. These books have either vertical or horizontal blank boxes in which you can fill out your plans. You'll need to determine what kind of setup you prefer, so shopping around will be important. There are many different sizes of lesson plan books, so find one that will best fit your needs. You can find these books at any local retail or online teacher store.

Pros: The biggest pro to using this type of planner is its ease of use (because it's already set up for you). It has bound pages, so the pages are more likely to stay in tact, and it is portable. With a clearly labeled cover and distinct design, it will also likely be easy to identify amid other materials on or around your desk.

Cons: One of the drawbacks to this type of planner is its lack of flexibility with the format. If, for example, you want lots of details or time delineations, you'll have to add those by hand each week to your lesson plans (whereas with a custom computer-created lesson plan, you can fill in those details yourself once and won't need to add them to your lesson plan each week).

Computer-Generated Lesson Plans

For many teachers, the idea of a computer-generated lesson plan format is appealing. With this format, you have the ability to add much more detail beforehand (once you know your schedule), and you can type in specific times for classes and other activities such as lunch, recess, or a study period. Simply type *teacher lesson plan template* into a search engine and you get hundreds of thousands of hits. You may need to search around a bit for a template that aligns with how you want to structure your lesson plans, but this may be a good route for you if you don't want to create your own format. If you feel competent in creating a lesson plan on the computer, there are many ways to do so. Some teachers use a simple word document or spreadsheet format and create boxes with rows and columns for the different subjects they teach. This may be something to experiment with over a weekend or through the summer when you have more time to try out different formats.

Pros: The major benefit to using this format is that it allows for you to customize as needed. You can add many different time slots or periods, class times, a "notes" section, or other reminders such as a weekly meeting, or a "specials" area to track students who leave the room at specific times. You can make the spaces or boxes as large or as small as you desire to give you enough space to write your plans.

Cons: One of the drawbacks to this format is the time it takes to create it. If you are using a template you find on the Internet, you'll still need to adapt it to meet your needs. If you are creating one yourself, you will need time to add appropriate sections or boxes, along with time slots for classes or other activities. Another drawback is that you will need to determine how to store these lesson plan sheets. You will likely need to three-hole punch them and place them in a binder, which could become somewhat cumbersome.

Other Considerations for Lesson Plan Formats

- Ask your colleagues for help. Often, colleagues will be more than happy to share their lesson plan template with you. If they agree to send their format to you electronically, you can use it as is or change it to meet your preferences.
- Many teachers (myself included) like to incorporate specific aspects of the day (like subject areas, special areas, morning procedures, and dismissal routines) within the actual lesson plan. It may take a bit of thinking and planning to discover which type of lesson plan works for you, but after you have an idea of how you want to structure your plans, you'll be well on your way to creating effective lessons.

Revising Your Lesson Format

It's important to reflect on your lesson plan format at least once a year to determine if the current layout is working and whether the elements of the lesson plan are efficient for next year's teaching structure. Sometimes I decide to change my lesson plan format based on a change in my schedule or the subjects I am teaching the following year. Other times, I've found that changing some aspect of the lesson plan format helps me to plan more appropriately for my lessons. For example, in recent years, I changed my computer-generated lesson plan from a vertical format to a horizontal layout, which provides a bit more room for me to write within the subject area boxes. I also created a small box at the top of each day's lesson plan for a "notes" section, as well as a "to-do" box on the right-hand side so I could jot reminders for meetings, things to copy, or materials to get ready for the day's lessons. Taking time to reflect and alter your lesson plan format from year to year is good practice. Having an effective, well-designed lesson plan promotes efficiency and contributes to an overall organized plan for the year.

> It's important to reflect on your lesson plan format at least once a year to determine if the current layout is working and whether the elements of the lesson plan are efficient for next year's teaching structure.

PLANNING FOR A SUBSTITUTE

When making effective weekly lesson plans, you also need to prepare and keep a substitute teacher folder handy for days when you are absent. This folder should include current information, as well as any forms or information that will help a guest teacher perform duties more efficiently. The more information you provide for a substitute teacher, the better chance you have of the day going smoothly. No matter the grade level you teach, there is much to do in a given day, so it's important to provide lots of details for the substitute, as well as list extra activities for students to do in case they have extra time at the end of an assignment or lesson. Here are some suggestions for what to include in your substitute teacher folder:

Components of a Substitute Folder

Copy of your lesson plan for the day. In writing a substitute lesson plan, be sure to include as much information as possible. My view about days when I am absent is that the guest teacher needs to carry out effective instruction and follow my plans well. I don't provide fluff assignments or busywork when a substitute teacher comes. There are routines to honor and much to teach every day, so I keep the day much the same for the substitute as I would if I were there. Because of the amount of information I want to communicate to the substitute teacher, I always type my plans. Typing allows me to add much more detail than if I were to write the plans by hand. Yes, they often end up being several pages long, but I've found that substitute teachers appreciate more information than less. Having been a substitute teacher, I can attest to appreciating the time that teachers took to explain not only procedures for lessons, but also for routines and classroom expectations. Most teachers can type much more quickly than write, and typed lessons are easier to read.

> Having an effective, well-designed lesson plan promotes efficiency and contributes to an overall organized plan for the year.

If you type (and save) your lesson plans for a substitute, you can copy and paste general portions of the plans when you are getting ready for another substitute at a different time of the year. You can also easily add information to your lesson plans as needed as you plan for your absence. If you are absent due to sickness, it's also a good idea to type your lesson plans so you can send them in an attachment to school personnel to ensure that the substitute gets a timely, detailed lesson plan. Be sure to ask your colleague to verify she received your lesson plans for the substitute.

Class lists. Be sure to include an accurate class list of all the classes you teach so your substitute has the most up-to-date information.

Seating charts. Be sure to leave a current seating chart for your classes so your substitute can call on students by name.

Lunch count and/or attendance forms or instructions for these procedures.

Medical concerns list. Include any medical or allergy information in your substitute folder. As mentioned in Chapter 6, you can use the Important Student Medical Information form on page 209 in the appendix to log important information for the substitute.

Procedures lists. Include a copy of school or district procedures for fire drills, tornado drills, or lock-downs. Remember to provide copies of class lists for these drills as well, or indicate where these class lists can be found in your classroom.

Tips for classroom procedures. These include arrival, departure, and discipline policies.

Extra activities. Keep a list of activities for students to do if they get done early with assignments (and include a set or two of "extra" worksheets or activities along with your lesson plans).

Substitute feedback form. Feedback is important and will help you understand how the day went while you were gone, as well as give you ideas for how to help future substitutes. The appendix includes a template for a Substitute Feedback Form on page 216.

There are some other considerations when preparing for a substitute teacher. First, it's a good idea to buy a substitute folder. Scholastic and Carson-Dellosa are two companies that manufacture these types of folders, and they can be found at any local teacher store or online. These folders provide space on the inside pockets to write important class procedures; ways to get student attention; information about your discipline policy, bathroom and hallway procedures; and more. Be sure to keep the information current. If you make changes from year to year, be sure to buy a new substitute folder. In addition, it's always a good idea to include a set of emergency lesson plans within your substitute folder. Although you will want your substitute to follow your carefully planned lesson, have this emergency plan in place in case you cannot provide detailed lesson plans when you are sick or have a family emergency. Having a well-crafted emergency plan in your substitute folder ensures that your substitute teacher will be able to carry out effective instruction for the duration of your absence.

Keys to Effective Lesson Planning

- ☐ Carve out structured time for planning lessons.
- ☐ Focus on one subject area or content area at a time while you are doing your lesson plans.
- ☐ Have materials and resources handy when planning for the week ahead.
- ☐ Create a yearly curriculum plan at the beginning of each school year.
- ☐ Know your curriculum so your plans are effective and efficient.
- ☐ Be sure to include necessary components for good lesson plans:
    - Include a list of materials
    - Provide details about lesson procedures
- ☐ Consider your personality when deciding on a lesson plan format.
- ☐ Be sure to have a well-organized substitute folder. Include:
    - Lesson plans for the day
    - Class lists
    - Seating charts
    - Lunch count and/or attendance forms
    - Medical concerns list
    - Procedures for fire drills, tornado drills, or lock-downs
    - Tips for classroom procedures
    - List of activities for students who finish assignments early
    - Substitute feedback form

10: Managing Technology

"I have not failed. I've just found ten thousand ways that won't work."
— Thomas Edison

When teachers hear the word technology, it brings up a whole host of emotions. On one hand, we love the abilities and educational opportunities afforded by technology. We can promote deeper research with our students than ever before. We can initiate more creative projects and collaboration. We can develop a more concise, elaborate communication system with other staff, parents, and even students, using e-mail, websites, blogs, podcasts, and more. We can do so much more with the advent of technology.

But on the other hand, technology carries with it some notes of negativity as well. Why? For one thing, it's one more thing on teachers' proverbial plates. The advancement of technology promotes many positive opportunities, but it also allows for teachers to become discouraged and disheartened. Truly, how do we fit everything in? That question lies at the center of many discussions I've had with teachers through the years. It's a very real and important question to seriously consider and plan for appropriately.

> We shouldn't use technology just to say we've used it. Being tech savvy may improve our clout with colleagues, but at the end of the day, what really matters is greater, deeper student learning.

The key is to stay positive, as demonstrated by Thomas Edison's quote at the start of this chapter. In thinking about technology, teachers also need to think about the word "balance." A good friend of mine put it into perspective when he said, "Everyone…don't panic. Technology is here. Everybody…just relax." No, this friend of mine isn't a teacher, but he is wise in that he knows how technology can be extremely helpful in accomplishing a wide variety of tasks—tasks that otherwise could not be as thoroughly performed. But we need to draw a line here. We shouldn't use technology just to say we've used it. Being tech savvy may improve our clout with colleagues, but at the end of the day, what really matters is greater, deeper student learning. So how do we get there? What aspects of technology do we need to consider for both ourselves and our students, while also keeping learning the top priority in the classroom?

E-MAIL

At school, e-mail is largely a teacher's tool, but I want to start with this topic. What did we ever do without it? In a typical busy day, it is possible to send dozens of e-mails and receive at least this many in your inbox. E-mail is invaluable for communicating with many different people on any given day. We may use e-mail to ask a secretary about paperwork, inform our guidance counselor about a student concern, pose an inquiry to our custodian about a broken desk, clarify with another teacher about a schedule glitch, or remind parents of important upcoming dates. This does not even begin to explain the extent to which we use e-mail to communicate. Teaching well requires a lot of communication with many different people. How do we navigate all of this and keep track of everything? How do we manage our time with e-mail and prevent it from taking over large parts of our day? Before we talk about time management, let's address some structures for organizing our e-mail system so we can use this tool in the most efficient way.

> E-mail is invaluable for communicating with many different people on any given day.

E-mail Folders

Although schools have different e-mail systems, you will probably have the capability to create various folders to contain separate categories of e-mails. One of my colleagues creates a folder within her e-mail system for each student in her class. When she communicates with a parent, she can drag and drop each e-mail into the folder for that child. This serves two purposes. First of all, anytime she wants to access information about parent communication, she can simply open the appropriate folder in her e-mail. Second, she can readily find all communication about each child in one spot instead of scrolling endlessly through an entire inbox for an e-mail. You could always use the "search" or "filter" button to help navigate various students' names or perhaps the subject line of an e-mail, but all too often, this is a fruitless effort. It is a powerful resource to be able to go directly to a student's name within your e-mail and locate any and all e-mail communications related to that child. You are working a bit harder initially because you have to take the time to create the folders and move the e-mails into them, but this initial effort will save you time in the future. This is one example of using technology wisely.

> It is a powerful resource to be able to go directly to a student's name within your e-mail and locate any and all e-mail communications related to that child.

What are some other folders you can create within your e-mail system? This depends largely on your grade level and perhaps what subject(s) you teach. For instance, you might want to have a folder for only grade-level e-mails (or even a folder for each teacher on your grade level team). You can also create folders for e-mails pertaining to various subjects, units, or projects. These folders simplify the process of finding specific e-mails. For instance, let's say you have a long unit dealing with the American Revolution. Perhaps you had a lot of parent inquiries about various assignments, projects, assessments, or even guest speakers. By designating an e-mail folder for that topic, you will always know where to find correspondence about this unit. You'll have only one place to look instead of having to search through several folders.

I also like creating folders specific to the district committees on which I serve. This is extremely beneficial because I need to access information on a regular basis for these committees, and having all the e-mails in one place helps me when I need to refer back to them to determine due dates, meeting days and times, and procedures related to the committee position.

Parent Address Groups

E-mail can be used as a solid communication tool with parents. While I still believe that talking in person or by phone with parents promotes the best chance for understanding, relating, and communicating clearly with each other, e-mail is a tremendous tool for keeping parents aware of calendar items, school events, general reminders, and concerns and praise dealing with your students. The good news is that e-mail is relatively universal, in the sense that most families have at least one account. However, some families may be limited in their ability to access or use e-mail on a regular basis, so I recommend sending hard copies of e-mails home with students on a regular basis. Print these off either the day you send the e-mail or the day after you send it. If you plan to communicate with parents via e-mail, briefly mention your plan at your school's open house, and ask the parents to provide contact information and indicate whether e-mail is a viable communication method for them. You can use the Parent Questionnaire on page 217 in the appendix to gather this important information.

> Some families may be limited in their ability to access or use e-mail...send hard copies of e-mails home with students on a regular basis.

Here are few tips for creating parent address groups:

- In order to add parents to your parent address group, you'll need to ask them for their e-mail addresses. There are a couple of ways to do this. During the first week of school, send home a note with your e-mail address in it and ask parents to e-mail you. With this method, you can easily and accurately capture their e-mail addresses by opening the e-mails they send, copying their addresses from the e-mails and pasting them into your address book. Another way is to ask parents to fill out their e-mail addresses on a form during a meet-and-greet or walk-through before school, or perhaps during an open house or curriculum night event.

With this method, you have a good chance of gathering most of your parents' e-mail addresses at one time, and you can enter them all at once rather than a little at a time.

- There are different ways to create groups in an e-mail system. Various e-mail systems generally have the terms "create

Communicating With Parents via E-mail

- Send frequent updates about important dates to remember.

- Provide quick reminders about a future field trip, materials that students need for projects, upcoming tests/quizzes, or an upcoming meeting at your school or within the district.

- Send quick notes of praise to parents about their children.

- Inform parents about a new unit of study to provide background information and relevant practice activities.

- Send web links to parents dealing with informative and current research about various educational issues.

- Attach your weekly/monthly parent letter.

- Inform parents of general minor concerns (recess-, friendship- or homework-related), but leave incidents of a more serious nature to a phone call or in-person meeting.

- Send attachments of important papers as needed. This could include study guides, project guidelines, and study advice.

a new contact," "create a new mail list," or "create a new card" to initiate the process of creating targeted mailing lists or contact groups.

- If you don't know how to create, use, and manage specific parent group folders with your current e-mail system, contact a fellow colleague or technology specialist who can help you navigate this important communication resource tool.

USING THE INTERNET

Entire books are written about how to use the Internet for a variety of purposes, not just in the field of education, but for just about any career or job. The Internet is a wide-open portal for students to explore, research, gain knowledge, compose, create, and present. How you incorporate the Internet in the classroom will vary a great deal based on the curriculum standards for your district, as well as the grade level and subject(s) you teach. Some districts have very specific technology standards for each grade level, so deciding how to use the Internet may be more prescribed for some teachers than others. Using the Internet in your curriculum can be both intimidating and exciting at the same time, so be proactive in thinking about when to do it. Here are some specific tips for using the Internet in your classroom:

- Determine into which study units you would like to incorporate using the Internet.
- Think about how you can incorporate a new Internet tool within an existing unit of study. Carefully evaluate the tool's usefulness with respect to the content you are teaching.
- Provide clear expectations for the care of computers and other electronic equipment in your classroom.
- Give good directions about navigating websites. For younger children, in the primary grades especially, take time to bookmark a site so they do not have to type a web address in the browser or try to search for it. Save yourself

some time later by investing a bit of time before you present your lesson.

- Provide students with step sheets if applicable (especially for detailed assignments or projects) or if there are several different steps you want students to follow.
- Be sure you or your district has developed parent permission forms for students to utilize the Internet. Also, remind students of their responsibility to tell you immediately of any inappropriate content they encounter while on the Internet.

KEEPING CURRENT WITH TECHNOLOGY

It's difficult to determine appropriate and current ways to activate student learning about technology without first learning about the technology yourself. Although teachers vary significantly in their level of understanding and training with the ever-changing tool that is technology, we need to engage in frequent opportunities for teacher training in this important area of our curriculum. You will never feel like you have learned it all when it comes to technology because technology doesn't stand still. It is always advancing. Even when you take time to learn about the newest software, read about the latest technology, or consider the newest gadgets, the technology will become somewhat obsolete within a year, or even a few months, because newer software and devices enter the education world.

> You will never feel like you have learned it all when it comes to technology because technology doesn't stand still. It is always advancing.

The good news about technology is that our students are often the ones who can best educate us about the websites, software, programs, or gadgetry we are trying to introduce within our lessons in meaningful ways. The combined learning experiences that can occur from a shared teaching experience with our students gives us perspective. Involving students this way promotes a willingness to allow students to showcase their knowledge and become more active participants in their learning.

For a teacher, the key to dealing with technology is to be willing to educate yourself and keep an open mind about trying new things. Take classes from time to time, read up on new technology efforts in the classroom, follow relevant blogs, ask for demonstrations or lessons from a district or building technology specialist, and be open to learning along with your students about the multitude of benefits technology can provide as you carry out instruction during the school year.

Remember to maintain a sense of balance with technology. Many teachers feel that if they don't initiate multiple projects, incorporate technology in every subject area, and jump on every technology bandwagon, they are not good teachers. This is not true. Take things one at a time. Carefully study your district standards for technology, and begin to implement activities or projects one unit at a time. It may not be perfect the first time around, but technology rarely is. Trying new things with technology promotes confidence in later projects. Here are some ideas for using the Internet with students:

> For a teacher, the key to dealing with technology is to be willing to educate yourself and keep an open mind about trying new things.

- Have students do research on a topic of interest pertaining to a unit of study within your content area.
- Ask students to research and then create a biography project on key individuals related to a content area or unit of study.
- Initiate lessons on using the Internet for various purposes, and then incorporate presentation skills into these projects. Students can use programs such as PowerPoint or Keynote to develop a project and present information to the class about their assigned topic.

- For a change of pace, have students participate in an interactive activity such as a WebQuest. This educational practice, developed in the 1990s, is an inquiry-learning activity in which students read and complete a variety of tasks (usually online) about a specific topic or subject. WebQuests usually involve a wider range of thinking skills, so this can be a good avenue for students to apply their learning. If you decide to initiate WebQuests in your classroom, be sure to use ones that clearly match your content area standards.
- Have students show their learning in a variety of ways by initiating a class blog or wiki. At the time of this book's printing, using blogs and wikis is a relatively new idea within classroom instruction. Set up a basic classroom blog, and ask students to respond to a variety of prompts or discussions. Students become highly motivated when they can access technology, write their thoughts about a particular topic, and view and comment on others' thoughts and reactions. Even kids who otherwise may not be keen on writing become more motivated due to the interactive nature of the activity and the use of technology to communicate ideas. Or set up a wiki, which is basically a website that involves students contributing their knowledge about a topic. The website's pages change as students alter or add and delete content. Using this technology tool promotes a sense of ownership and empowers students to feel that they are experts about a variety of topics. You can also utilize a wiki to provide specific information about class procedures or to describe your

Carefully study your district standards for technology, and begin to implement activities or projects one unit at a time. It may not be perfect the first time around, but technology rarely is.

program to parents. Lots of resources are available to learn more about how to incorporate a class wiki, blog, or podcast into your classroom. See the Suggested Reading List on page 204 in the appendix for some ideas.

Keep an Idea File

As you learn more about technology, you'll no doubt come across a variety of ideas you may want to implement into your curriculum at one time or another. You might find an interesting article about a particular program or website that could be used creatively in your classroom to promote deeper learning. You might identify a particular program or website that you could incorporate into a unit of study to enhance student motivation and individual creativity or perhaps group collaboration. Create a folder to contain interesting articles about ideas for projects, programs, or websites you'd like to consider. You can look to this idea file for ways to keep stretching yourself to incorporate technology in meaningful ways with your students. Be open to thinking creatively about how to use technology in your grade level and within your content area(s). While searching online, be sure to bookmark helpful websites that provide timely information about how to incorporate technology into lessons.

TIME MANAGEMENT

Like everything else in the classroom, all teachers must be master managers of time. Nearly each minute of your day is spoken for, so the activities and tasks you perform for yourself (and for your students, most importantly) must be worthwhile. While it's great to be creative in incorporating technology in various ways, the technology must have purpose and meaning for curriculum and should stimulate students toward problem solving, critical thinking, questioning, and inquiry. The same is true for how you use your time during planning periods or before or after school. Though using e-mail is an incredible avenue for saving time and communicating with a multitude of people about countless topics, it can no doubt swallow up precious time for planning lessons, organizing supplies and materials, grading papers, or meeting with a colleague to discuss a child's performance. It's true that in every profession, employees must deal with the challenge of managing time well, but teachers especially need to be critically aware of the time they spend, think about how they can maintain or increase productivity, and work to balance technology to ensure creative, genuine learning experiences for their students.

E-mail

In thinking about time management and e-mail, take time to determine parameters for yourself. You might decide to check e-mail two or three times a day, and then stick to that schedule. Because parents and staff often send messages that need immediate attention, it is not uncommon for teachers to check e-mail several times per day. Doing so is both manageable and smart, but keep in mind that you don't want e-mail to become a distraction from your work.

> When you can't immediately respond to any e-mail, flag the e-mail in your inbox so that you will remember to return to it at a later time.

When possible, you should respond to e-mails immediately or as quickly as possible. Otherwise, you may forget to respond altogether, or you could end up with a backlog of e-mails to which you need to respond, and you will spend a lot of time all at once to catch up. When you can't immediately respond to an e-mail, flag the e-mail in your inbox so you will remember to return to it at a later time. You can either mark the message as unread, flag an e-mail response to send later, or keep a running list of e-mails on a to-do list that you need to answer.

You can also initiate some preferences within your e-mail system that will save you time. For instance, most e-mail systems allow for a preview pane or partial e-mail to show up so you can quickly scan the contents of your e-mails. This is helpful in identifying the importance of your e-mails, which allows you to determine which e-mails need immediate responses.

CLEARING COMPUTER CLUTTER

It's great to embark on utilizing technology in a multitude of ways as a teacher. Being able to use e-mail quickly, navigate the Internet efficiently, and create documents, projects, and activities on the computer can enhance our performance as teachers as well as student learning. Learning to use various programs, software, and websites within your curriculum are important aspects of keeping current with today's technology.

But just as you need to be aware of methods for organizing your paperwork, you also need to manage files and documents on your computer, or you risk having a cluttered desktop where none of your files are organized. Having a cluttered desktop on your computer or within your files on your hard drive can be stressful. When accessing your computer you want to be able to find what you need, click on it, and go from there. You don't want to spend ten minutes searching for a file, only to realize you aren't even sure what you titled it in the first place. Follow these tips to help you cut down on the clutter on your computer:

> Just as you need to be aware of methods for organizing your paperwork, you also need to manage files and documents on your computer, or you risk having a cluttered desktop.

Keep a Clean Desktop

Create subject-specific folders on your desktop (or within a documents folder on your hard drive). Then you can specify where to save a document. If you are creating a math vocabulary worksheet, be sure to save it in the Math folder. If you are creating a Getting to

Know You survey, perhaps you can create a folder entitled "Beginning of the Year." The type and number of folders you create depends on your grade level and the content areas you teach (as well as how narrow you want the categories for your computer folders to be).

Manage Your Inbox

E-mail can pile up quickly, and before you know it, you can have hundreds of e-mails sitting in your inbox. Some teachers are efficient at deleting e-mails, but other teachers (myself included) do better with a set time to go through and clean out e-mails. If possible, try to keep your inbox clear so only new, unread messages are in it. If you don't need to reference the message again, delete it as soon as you read it. If the e-mail contains important information about dates or times for an event, immediately transfer that information to your calendar. Then delete the e-mail or move it to a folder related to the event. If you need to reply to an e-mail, move it to a Drafts folder. After you reply, delete the e-mail or move it to a subject-specific folder. A clear inbox eliminates distractions and means you have filed important e-mails in other folders and deleted unimportant messages.

Just like purging your paper files, you want your computer files to contain only those things that are useful, current, and relevant to your curriculum and teaching life.

Regularly Purge Computer Files

You should also go through the folders and files on your computer on a regular basis. It's hard to set a number of times to do this cleaning-out session through the year, but I recommend doing so at least once or twice a year so it doesn't become an overwhelming task. Go through your folders and identify any documents that are outdated or not useful, and delete them. Although individual files usually do not take up a lot of space (unless you've included lots of pictures or clip art), multiple files do eventually eat up the available space on your computer. Just like purging your paper files, you want your computer files to contain only those things that are useful, current, and relevant to your curriculum and teaching life. Although purging computer files may pale in importance compared to the priority

Technology Tips and Tricks

- ☐ Create and use various e-mail folders to organize important e-mails. Create folders for individual students, parent groups, projects, and units of study.

- ☐ Provide opportunities for parents to receive hard copies of e-mail communications, and be sensitive to parents' diverse capacities for dealing with technology.

- ☐ Use e-mail to communicate with parents in creative, meaningful ways about important dates, general reminders, individual student praise, and links to relevant educational websites.

- ☐ Think creatively about using the Internet within your classroom. Determine units or topics that support using various programs.

- ☐ Give clear directions for navigating websites (provide step sheets if necessary). Ensure that you have a current parent permission form on file for Internet use.

- ☐ Stay current in learning about newer technology applications. Take courses, follow blogs, and ask knowledgeable staff to mentor you in learning how to use various programs.

- ☐ Be willing to make mistakes the first time you try a program, Internet activity, or presentation application. Use these experiences to build confidence.

you need to place on good teaching practices, your computer is also an extremely important teaching tool that requires effort and time in order for it to be a relevant, helpful tool long term.

- ☐ Keep an idea file for technology, and try to incorporate at least one new program or project within your curriculum each semester. Remember to purge your idea file from time to time because technology information becomes outdated quickly.

- ☐ Think about how to manage your time well in using technology in your classroom.

- ☐ Take time to periodically purge e-mails and computer files. The more organized you are with your computer, the more motivated and encouraged you'll be to use it in multiple ways for classroom projects.

- ☐ Always have a back-up plan when using technology. While technology can be a teacher's best friend, you never know when the Internet may be down, when the server just isn't responding, or when the power will go out. Think ahead and plan alternate activities so you can still provide meaningful learning in these unfortunate, but realistic, possible circumstances.

11: Managing Your Day

"Better three hours
too soon than a
minute too late."
— William Shakespeare

As a teacher, you absolutely must become an excellent manager of your day. It is one of the most critical aspects of maintaining your sanity on the job. Balancing what you do each day—instructing students, maintaining order on your desk, communicating with colleagues and parents, managing e-mail, and so much more—seems like a daily battle in many respects. Managing your day well requires a great deal of planning. This chapter will provide valuable information about how to maintain a sense of calm despite the hurried, stressful pace of a typical day.

PLANNING FOR TOMORROW

How do you leave your desk at the end of the day? Is it organized? Messy? Somewhat tidy? What steps do you take to organize for the next school day? One of the best ways to create a sense of order even before starting another school day is to focus on leaving your room—and especially your desk—tidy and organized. Being organized and prepared for the next day starts at the end of the previous day. Your desk is your working hub for paperwork, lesson plans, teacher manuals, mail, worksheets, and office supplies, so it is essential to keep this space organized.

> One of the best ways to create a sense of order even before starting another school day is to focus on leaving your room—and especially your desk—tidy and organized.

Preparing Your Desk

During a given day, my desk can get pretty messy. It is quite maddening sometimes, because my inner organizing "gene" very much wants to kick in when I notice some papers and piles encroaching on my desk or a table in the room. But, over time, I've been able to change my thinking by remembering that the time I spend with my students is for teaching and instructing. I now realize that these piles can wait...for a bit. At the end of the day, I always attack my desk, organizing every piece of mail and every stack of papers. I established a daily routine for organizing my desk, and this routine helps me ensure it is well ordered and leaves me feeling calm. Most teachers already do this to some degree, but perhaps it's tempting to say, "Oh, I'll get everything ready in the morning." The more prepared you are in organizing your desk the night before, the better. Another benefit to keeping a clean and organized desk is that you'll walk into the room the next day and see how orderly and functional your desk is. This alone will likely provide some initial energy and motivation for the day ahead.

> Another benefit to keeping a clean and organized desk is that you'll walk into the room the next day and see how orderly and functional your desk is. This alone will likely provide some initial energy and motivation for the day ahead.

Tips for Preparing Papers and Materials

There are numerous steps you can take to ensure that your paperwork and materials are organized for the next day's instruction. Use these tips as a guide at the end of the day to keep your desk orderly and prepared for the next day:

- Determine the worksheets you need for the next day and place them, in order, on your desk. (Some teachers even place their worksheets in separate file folders or trays designating paperwork for each day of the upcoming week. See Chapter 7 for more information about using a weekly file sorter.)
- Locate and gather all materials and supplies for the next day's lessons, and place them in an accessible location. Even if you still need to review the proper use of them or possibly count the materials out for the number of students the next day, at least you'll have the materials set out and ready to go.
- Determine what papers you need to take home, and put them in your bag for grading.

- Set your lesson plans on top of your desk so they are ready for you (or for a substitute in an emergency situation) the next day.
- Write yourself a sticky note for things you need to remember first thing in the morning, and place the note on your desk or your computer in a highly visible spot so you will not forget. (I often do this when I have a special meeting to attend first thing in the morning.)
- Look over your schedule or weekly planner to determine any upcoming special assemblies or activities so you are prepared ahead of time. Be sure you know start and end times.

It may be helpful to review Chapter 5 to help you identify various methods for keeping your desk space organized and tidy.

Ready Materials and Supplies

It's important to use your lesson plans as a place to record what materials you will need. A to-do list section within your lesson plans is one place to write reminders about supplies or materials you need to acquire. This section or list should be one of the first things you refer to in planning your day.

Sometimes readying your materials for lessons can be a hassle, especially because some supplies are hard to come by, and you may sometimes have to go on a hunt around the school (or school district) to locate what you need. Try to locate and gather all necessary materials for future lessons well in advance (at least several days ahead of time) so you are not caught off guard. Certainly, no amount of planning will provide perfect results (no matter how hard you try), and sometimes you simply cannot account for every single thing you need, but the beauty of a well-crafted lesson plan is that you will know ahead of time what materials you need to teach a lesson well.

PREPARE FOR THE DAY AHEAD

Here are some ideas that will help you start your day in an organized way so you are ready for everything you have planned:

Creating Prep Time

I've found that proper planning is the most helpful ingredient toward making my daily lessons go well and empowering me to connect learning material with my students. When I take dedicated, quiet, structured time before school to study the upcoming day's lessons and determine exactly what steps I need to take to carry out these lessons, I am so much happier with the end result. It helps me achieve my main job—ensuring meaningful student learning. I never want to be the kind of teacher that "flies by the seat of her pants" during a lesson (thankfully I think this kind of teacher is the exception, not the rule). Of course, from time to time, some lessons allow for a more open, relaxed feeling. However, there is a still a great deal of planning that goes into any type of class lesson, so being prepared is the key.

> The beauty of a well-crafted lesson plan is that you will know ahead of time what you need in to teach a lesson well.

Let me first say that a teacher's morning time is precious, and often teachers have meetings on one or more days of the week, so this time can be very limited. Be sure to account for all of the day's responsibilities and arrive early enough to fully prepare for the day ahead. On some days when I have morning meetings, I plan to arrive at school even just fifteen minutes earlier to carve out some prep time for my day ahead. So what steps should you take to create this prep time? First, you need to consider how much time it takes to ready yourself for your day. If you followed the advice in Chapter 9, you've probably already completed your lesson plan for that day ahead of time. Your morning prep time is when you can fine tune and solidify what you are doing during your immediate lessons for the day. Think through each lesson and ensure that you have a handle on the flow of activities. Consider what you will do first, second, and so on.

It's important to consider how you can create more time to do accurate work within your day and ensure that lesson plans are sound.

Your morning prep time is a good opportunity to shut your door and do some solitary work. Isolating yourself in the morning can be difficult because sometimes you need time to say hello to your colleagues and feel grounded for the day ahead. Chapter 9 outlines some time-management principles. It's important to consider how you can create more time to do accurate work within your day and ensure that lesson plans are sound. Making a concerted effort to block out distractions, to ensure that all of your proverbial ducks are in a row, provides a more successful result. This is certainly a better alternative to winging a lesson, which would reduce your ability to teach well. This focused time will allow you to get centered and ready yourself for the day.

I usually find that sitting down at my desk and taking the time to study my plans is the best place to start. I begin by looking at my first class of the day and considering important guiding questions. Here are some questions you might ask yourself as you consider your upcoming day with students:

- Do I understand the objective(s) for the lesson? Have I determined how best to communicate the objective(s) to the students?
- Have I marked the exact page number(s) I'll be referencing with students?
- Have I familiarized myself with the concept or specific directions of the assignment(s) so I can explain them carefully to the students?
- Do I have content area vocabulary posted or ready to share with students?

- Do I have all materials ready and counted out?
- Do I know how to use and incorporate all of the materials for the lesson?
- Have I decided on the due date for the assignment?
- Will there be a scoring guide or rubric for this assignment (if so, have I shared this rubric ahead of time with students)?
- How many points will this assignment be worth?

Some of these questions may seem a bit basic, especially for veteran teachers who already initiate this kind of reflection somewhat automatically prior to the day's lessons, but even with my years of experience, I've found that it's still good practice to review a list like this daily to determine the exact objectives and lesson procedures for the day. Reflecting in this manner helps me feel prepared and allows me to confidently present lessons to my students. Students can certainly ascertain when you are prepared (or not), and they can tell when you feel a strong command of your content (or not).

Students can sense your confidence, and they seem to pick up on your enthusiasm for lessons. All teachers want their students to be engaged and enthusiastic when it comes to learning. Though it takes a lot of work for teachers to step beyond just writing weekly lesson plans, it is also a great practice to take the time, on a daily basis, to prepare and think about what you are setting out to do with the day's lessons.

The Daily Checklist

When I have a high volume of activities during a given lesson, I find it helpful to jot a few quick notes to myself about what I'll be doing. These notes are a sort of checklist that I make in addition to (and based on) the weekly lesson plans I've already written. I can refer to these notes quickly as I am teaching, and they provide a sort of "ready reference" for what I need to do throughout the class period. This checklist idea is useful for teachers of any grade level, in any teaching configuration, from elementary to high school. One way to add this list to your lesson plan is to simply use a sticky note or small pad of paper. Simply jot down the major components of your lesson so your eye is drawn to what you need to do within your lesson. Here is an example list I wrote for an upcoming ninety-minute language arts class:

Inferring mini lesson

Read aloud

Independent reading/conferencing

Persuasive writing mini lesson

Graphic organizer/independent writing

Share time

These notes to myself, which took less than a minute to write down, were all I needed to help me structure a more successful lesson. I had already planned these activities and written them in my lesson plans several days prior, and I knew my objectives for the lesson as well. Quickly jotting down these activities in order helps my brain focus on the essential or core aspects of the day.

You can do this for any subject area(s) that you teach. If you teach four sections of the same subject area, you might need just one sticky note for your entire day. Or if different classes are at different points within a given lesson, write a separate sticky note for each class. If you are an elementary teacher, you could write two or three sticky notes for each subject area of the day. It's a great way to gather your thoughts and focus your mind on the day ahead, and it will keep you organized as you are bombarded with distractions throughout the day. If your lesson plans are rather detailed to begin with, you may find it easier to refer to (and transport) a simple sticky note. I know that I can always grab my lesson plans should I need to look at something in more detail as I am teaching.

CHECK YOUR DAILY SCHEDULE

One of the first things I do each day is check the day's activities as listed on my weekly schedule. At the beginning of the school year, I type a master schedule list of classes that typically occur on each day of the week, such as speech, ESL class, or classes in the resource or enrichment room. This schedule lets me know ahead of time which students go where, and at what time, as well as how many days per week this occurs. It's good practice to check this list every day so you can keep students updated about what they miss during a given lesson. It's also a good idea to have an assigned buddy in the classroom who can inform students of general information or lesson content they missed during a lesson or class period. You can use the General Weekly Schedule form on page 220 in the appendix to record information about your students' whereabouts throughout a given week.

Note that the activities I record on my master schedule list are different from specials, such as art, music, and physical education, that involve the entire class. I account for specials in my weekly lesson plans so I can schedule my instruction time around these classes during the week.

KEEP A DAILY TO-DO LIST

Teachers have a wide range of methods for recording their daily tasks. Most teachers choose to use a daily or weekly to-do list to remind them of what they need to accomplish. As you prepare for the day ahead, be sure to create or consult your to-do list. Sometimes the tasks on your list are mostly ones beyond the normal scope of the day. Here are some possible types of tasks you may need to add to your to-do list on any given day:

- Respond to an important e-mail or make phone calls
- Sign paperwork or send it to the office
- Speak to a staff member about a particular student
- Copy worksheets for a unit of study
- Fill out a student book order
- Complete a student survey or paperwork for an IEP
- Type up a worksheet related to an upcoming unit of study
- Organize certain supplies for tomorrow's lesson

- Gather some reading books for an ESL student
- Create a class chart for an upcoming lesson

Many times, my to-do list seems never ending, but once in a while, I may have only a few items on my list. I like having this list on my desk at all times, because I can look at it a few times a day, and if I notice I have even a few extra minutes, I can sometimes complete a task or two during this small window of time. If you're like me, you find it extremely satisfying to cross things off of a to-do list. My mom (who is a retired teacher) and I have laughed about how I sometimes add things to my to-do list that I have recently completed, just so I can cross off one or two additional things (she has a habit of doing this, too). It's great to feel a sense of accomplishment when there is so much to do during the busy week.

A to-do list keeps you grounded. Even if the list is long and might initially seem overwhelming, it is good to have everything written down. Taking time to be reflective and write down all of the tasks that need your attention can be cathartic in and of itself. Writing it down may not accomplish the actual task, but it is a step in the right direction.

You probably keep a running to-do list and may, therefore, refer to it as a list for the week. A good time to start a weekly to-do list is while you are planning lessons. As you plan, make a separate list of any tasks you'll need to accomplish to carry out those plans. After you finish planning lessons, review your calendar and schedule for the upcoming week, and think about any tasks you need to finish or deadlines you need to meet. Add these schedule-related items to your to-do list. If an item is time sensitive, place its due date next to it so you know how to prioritize it. If you know ahead of time you want to tackle a task on a specific day, note the day next to the task.

At the end of each day, consult your weekly to-do list and identify the items you need to or want to accomplish the next day. Be realistic about what you can accomplish so you set yourself up for success. Write these tasks on a separate, daily to-do list. If you accomplish all of them the next day, and you still have time, you can find another item or two on your weekly list to accomplish.

Remember, every minute of your day counts. If you are organized and have your to-do list handy, you can take full advantage of any extra time (even five minutes) instead of losing time trying to decide what to do next.

MANAGE DISTRACTIONS

Distractions are a normal part of a teacher's day. We often can breeze past these distractions with minor difficulty. But sometimes, when they occur in waves, distractions become hard to manage. It is imperative that teachers keep distractions to a minimum. Here are some frequent distractions—some of which we can control, and some of which we cannot control—and solutions to them:

Distraction: Fire and emergency drills

Solution: The best way to prepare for school fire and emergency drills is to keep and maintain current class lists in a prominent spot (preferably near the door) so you can grab them at a moment's notice. In addition, be sure to teach students ahead of time about proper procedures and expectations for fire and tornado drills.

Distraction: School personnel or parent visits

Solution: Maintain an organized calendar so you know if or when any individuals will be coming into your room. If you have a staff member or parent visit your room unexpectedly for an observation, remember that even if you're a bit nervous, your main purpose is to carry out your lesson plans. This way, you can work toward engaging students in your lesson to the best of your ability.

Distraction: Assemblies

Solution: Develop a strategic approach with your grade-level colleagues. If your grade-level team has an inordinate amount of work to do during a particularly busy week, you could arrange for one or two of the grade-level teachers to monitor the students during part of the assembly while others can be freed up to attend to other tasks. Halfway through (or at another school assembly later in the year), you can return the favor and watch the students for the remainder of the time.

Be sure to clear this with your building principal first so he or she is aware of your intentions. Although it is important and beneficial to attend most school assemblies or activities, it is sometimes also helpful to rethink the structure of a given day and creatively manage your time.

Distraction: Classroom interruptions

Classroom interruptions include announcements from the office, materials/supplies dropped off for students, students who deliver messages to you from another teacher and other teachers or staff coming into the classroom to talk with the teacher or an individual student.

Solution: Think about whether you can handle these distractions before or after school, rather than during the instructional part of the day with students. If so, make a note to revisit these issues at the end of the day and carry on with your instruction.

Distraction: Students leaving due to illness or appointments

Solution: Create an absent folder and task another student in the class with filling it out for the absent child. Another idea is to have a class buddy for each student. When a student is absent, his buddy will update him on lessons and class activities that occurred during his absence. You will likely want to follow through with that student upon his return, but assigning class buddies teaches students responsibility. When a student shares with his buddy what he missed the preceding day, he is also summarizing for himself what content he learned, which strengthens his own learning as well.

Distraction: E-mail notifications

Solution: Change the preferences in your e-mail system so you turn off the sound indicator for e-mail notifications (or keep the volume low). Though helpful in knowing when you get a new e-mail, this e-mail indicator sound can easily become a distraction for both you and your students. What's worse, if you go over to your computer to read the e-mail during instruction, you risk losing students' attention to the lesson in progress. You could, in effect, be communicating to students (even if this is not your intention) that checking your e-mail is more important than they are. Aim to check e-mail only a certain number of times per day.

Distraction: Building maintenance and construction or noise

Solution: Ask that your building's maintenance and janitorial staff contact you before they work in or near your room so you are aware of the situation ahead of time and can plan for this distraction appropriately. If the work is ongoing, make note of any breaks in the noise and take full advantage of this time.

Managing Aspects of Your Day

- [ ] Take time to organize your desk at the end of each workday. Maintain a routine for tidying and organizing your paperwork.

- [ ] Record pertinent information in your weekly lesson plans to indicate what you need to do each day to prepare for various activities or experiments.

- [ ] Lay out your worksheets for the next day in an orderly fashion so you are prepared.

- [ ] Ready materials and supplies at least the day before so you are prepared.

- [ ] Carve out prep time for yourself before school to fine tune your lesson plans and get focused for your upcoming day. Plan to arrive at school ten to fifteen minutes earlier than normal so you can allow for this important reflective time.

- [ ] Study your plans with a detailed eye. Ask specific, guiding questions to determine whether you are ready for the day ahead.

- [ ] Consider writing a quick daily checklist that indicates the major aspects of your daily lessons. Include specific information and key words that will give you a good feel for the general flow of the lessons.

- [ ] Keep a daily/weekly to-do list. Create a fresh list at the beginning of each week to keep tasks current.

- [ ] Determine creative ways to manage distractions. Think about how you can handle these distractions in positive ways, and reflect on how to eliminate distractions when possible.

12: Students in the Organized Classroom

"But everything should be done in a fitting and orderly way."

— 1 Corinthians 14:40
(New International Version)

TEACHING STUDENTS ABOUT BEING ORGANIZED

Strong organizing skills are one of the most important tools students need to be successful in school. This is not to say that without a sense of organization students will not be successful. Perhaps you know of peers from your own background who have become very successful adults despite their lack of organization. Some books even proclaim a sense of disorganization may be beneficial to some people. But in most circumstances, when students have simple, consistent systems for organizing, they will perform better in school. As you help students become more organized in the classroom, it is important to understand that children vary widely in their ability to organize their papers, materials, and supplies. Students seem to experience the process of being organized in a few distinct ways depending on their natural bent toward being organized, as well as what kind of support they receive from parents and teachers.

> Strong organizing skills are one of the most important tools students need to be successful in school.

Stages of Organization

Students' abilities for being organized tend to fall in three broad stages: organized by nature, transitional organizers, and organizationally challenged. While not labels, these stages can help you understand your students and identify effective ways to support them in their efforts toward being organized and successful.

Organized by Nature. These students seem to have an inherent sense of organization. They are adept at turning in work, placing papers in their proper spots, and finding what they need when they need it. Their materials are usually very well ordered, and they may be seen as super-neat in their organizing style. In my many years as an elementary teacher, I've noticed that many students in this category—both boys and girls—create organizing systems on their own or with some minor direction from a teacher or parent. After the system is in place, they are able to stick with it, adjusting it to make it work for their own personality. They are sometimes more detail-oriented and take a careful approach to most aspects of schooling.

Transitional Organizers. These students can generally find papers, turn in most homework, and locate materials when needed. What they may not have is a system in place that will guide them to stay organized. These students may have messier backpacks, desks, and folders, but they do seem to have a general sense of order that works for them most of the time. They may occasionally miss an assignment because of their somewhat disorganized style, but it is not usually a recurring problem. Periodically checking in with these students—either with an occasional planner check or by helping them sort out their desk, folder, or binder—is often all it takes to get them back on track.

Organizationally Challenged. The term "organizationally challenged" is not meant to denote that a student in this stage is unable to be organized, nor is it a negative connotation regarding a student's disposition or personality. It also does not refer to a character flaw. What it does mean is that students in this stage have wide and varied difficulties with organizing, and this affects their learning in some way. Students in this category are very unorganized and require outside help to get them back on track. They have yet to successfully create or use organizing systems for their schoolwork or storage of materials. Students in this category generally have trouble completing or turning in homework. They often lose papers and cannot remember where they put things, and they have no system for organizing their school papers or materials. Another important and often unknown characteristic about students within this stage is that they may or may not realize the depth of their disorganization. Some children may feel that it's "just the way they are." A teacher can guide a student in this category by setting up specific systems, such as signing off daily on the student's planner, meeting with the child weekly to organize and file papers, performing weekly desk checks, and having discussions about ways to stay organized. You may also want to ask parents to help with various tasks, such as checking their child's planner and homework each night. Occasional rewards for positive improvements may also be helpful, either at home or at school.

While teachers can be excellent role models in an authority setting, it is often the follow-through and the consistent guidance that parents provide that helps students remain organized.

Remember, these are simply stages, not permanent categories or labels. Students can progress from organizationally challenged to transitionally organized and possibly on to organized by nature with positive encouragement and guidance. You can create systems for students who lack them. Then check in weekly (or daily if needed) to ensure they are using the system. If a system just isn't working for a student, consider adjusting it to meet the student's specific needs. Ask the student what it is about the system that isn't working, and try to find a solution.

PARENTS AND THE ORGANIZING PROCESS

In addition to a child's natural organizational tendencies, many individuals contribute to a child's overall sense of organization. Teachers guide students' organizational systems in many ways at school, but parents also influence a child's organizational success to a large degree. While teachers can be excellent role models in an authority setting, it is often the follow-through and the consistent guidance that parents provide that helps students remain organized. Communicate with parents regularly about the systems you have for organizing, the supplies students should be using, and how parents can help at home. This open communication is key to bridging the connection between home and school. It may be helpful to include descriptions of your expectations for various organizational structures in a parent letter at the beginning of the year or in a handbook that you create for parents (perhaps you could discuss these important items during your open house or curriculum night). Put this information in print to help parents understand your expectations and methods for organizing student paperwork and to clearly outline procedures for transporting paperwork between home and school. It's also a good idea to provide a detailed explanation about the paperwork systems you expect students to utilize (such as a binder or an eight-pocket organizer) so parents can support their children in keeping these systems organized and tidy.

EXPECTATIONS AND CONSISTENCY WITH ORGANIZING

When students know and understand teachers' expectations within the classroom, they have a better chance for success, and they will be happier and more secure as well. Students must understand what their teacher expects of them, especially in regard to organizing their supplies and materials. Make your expectations for organization known from the first day of the school year. Most teachers, from primary through the high school level, dedicate a large part of the first few days of the new school year to working with students to set up binders and folders, label and organize supplies and materials in students' desks or lockers, and explain procedures and routines in the room that will promote a sense of structure and organization.

As a teacher, you will need to determine those structures and routines ahead of time so you can clearly communicate with students what you want them to do in a variety of circumstances. Usually teachers need to explain classroom expectations over a period of several days to prevent information overload and allow the students to absorb the information. You might plan to explain three or four organizational systems per day. A few initial systems you will need to consider early on in the year include:

> The more you remind students of how to organize, the more they will organize.

- How you want students to organize their homework
- How you want students to organize the papers they keep at school
- How you want students to organize the papers they take home
- Locations for storing materials
- Methods for transporting common supplies from room to room if students change classrooms throughout the day

The key to helping your students understand your systems for organizing (as well as their own systems) is consistency. To maintain consistency, you may find it helpful to write out your expectations and your systems before the start of the school year. Keep a copy of these expectations in your teacher reference binder and, if appropriate, consider posting it somewhere in the room so students can see it. Students usually do very well in maintaining our high expectations when we are clear about what we want. When we do not follow through or lack consistency in explaining or reinforcing those systems, it's natural for students to become confused. Students may not understand the form or function of a system you've set up if they are not using it consistently. Be sure your organizing systems make a positive contribution toward student learning, and dedicate time to reinforce how to maintain the system. Consistency breeds consistency. The more you remind students of how to organize, the more they will organize.

THE IMPORTANCE OF MAINTENANCE

Your careful classroom organizing plans won't last if you don't create time for regular maintenance of the system throughout the year. I admit, I sometimes need improvement in this area. I work hard to help students set up systems for organizing a whole host of supplies. Their binders are well kept, and their spiral notebooks are all labeled and used purposefully. Their supplies are labeled and stored well. But sometimes, in the midst of busy schedules, curriculum demands, interruptions, and just plain forgetfulness, I don't always take time to guide students in the process of maintaining this wonderful system that we've established. Often the students are the ones who inform me that we need to maintain order in our well-established binders and notebooks. A student may pipe up one day, saying, "Uh, Mrs. Unger, are we going to clean out our eight-pocket organizer soon?" I glance over, embarrassed to see that student's bulging organizer. Time won out in this particular instance, but students really do help guide us along in the organizing process. They become part of the consistency factor for organization. That's when you know you've done a relatively good job in setting expectations with your students; they know when it's time to perform some organizational task. I appreciate comments like, "Hey, Mrs. Unger, can we work on organizing the library soon?" or, "Can we empty our desks and clean them out soon?" because it means the system is working.

Cleaning Out Desks

Students' desks can become extensions of their personalities. Teachers can often determine a great deal about their students after a short period of time simply by observing how they keep their desks organized. It's important for students to feel as if they are in control of their space, but not at the expense of keeping materials, supplies, and paperwork organized and ordered within their desks. See Chapter 4 for specific tips and ideas to guide students to keep their desk spaces clean and organized.

Supply Checks

A proper supply of materials helps students perform well on a daily basis in school. Most teachers provide detailed supply lists at the beginning of the year, which allows students to start the year with everything they need. However, students use up these supplies throughout the year so it's important for teachers to do periodic check-ins to see whether students have all necessary supplies, especially concerning frequently used items such as notebooks, pencils, and pens. A few times a year, I pull our grade-level supply list and remind students of what's on the list. Sometimes I give them another copy of the list and ask them to highlight any supplies that are running low and circle any items they no longer have. Students take these lists home so their parents can replenish their supply and the students can continue to be prepared for instruction in various subject areas.

MAKING IT FUN

Let's face it, sometimes kids need some incentives to stay organized. They are learning in stages about the benefits of being organized, and they don't always know immediately how organizing can positively impact them. Help this process along by creatively inviting students to maintain their individual systems for organizing so the overall classroom remains well ordered. Here are a few tips for keeping kids motivated to stay organized:

The Desk Fairy and Other Prizes

Many teachers like to use specific awards to praise students when they consistently keep their materials or supplies organized. The Desk Fairy can award small treats (candy or otherwise) to students for keeping their desks clean. This type of award motivates many students who need help in this area, and those who already keep their desks clean get a nice side benefit as well. When you introduce the award, set specific guidelines that desks must meet in order to receive the award. This provides a consistent standard for the prize and helps students meet your expectations. Consider posting the guidelines to encourage students to keep their desks clean. Here are some parameters I give to my students:

- No loose papers in your desk
- Books, binders, and spirals must be stacked neatly in your desk

- No visual clutter (like toys or gadgets)
- No unnecessary materials or supplies in your desk (only the basics!)

Another motivational idea is to use a special word or quote that you add letters to on a chalkboard or whiteboard to visually show when students do well with a certain task. For instance, I like to use the word *rewards*. Each time students show good behavior, excellent work habits, or just generally have a stellar day, I will write a letter on the board. Students work toward spelling this word on the board, and after they spell *rewards*, they can vote on a special class reward, such as an extra recess, extra computer time, or a longer reading period (called a "Read-In" at our school). Students love working for these types of rewards. Another approach is to add marbles or candy to a class jar. After the marbles or candy fills the jar, students get a special prize as a reward.

The Importance of Specific Praise

Sometimes all it takes for students to continue with habits for organizing is to give them praise from time to time. Specific praise is best. Rather than simply saying, "I like your neat desk," you can indicate what you like about their desk. You can say, "I really liked seeing your books stacked neatly, and I really appreciate that you take the time to put all of your papers in your organizer. This shows responsibility." Just as adults appreciate the power of specific words related to positive job performance, kids need and deserve our specific praise for a job well done.

Supporting Students' Organization Skills

☐ Remember that as individuals, students come into your classroom with varying abilities for organizing. They can be organized by nature, or perhaps they are transitional organizers. They may also be organizationally challenged. Learning this information about your students early on will give you a good perspective about how you can help them.

☐ When possible, enlist parent support. The more you communicate your expectations for organizing systems, the better.

☐ Set clear expectations for how you want students to be organized. Be consistent with the systems you establish, and give students clear directions for organizing within these systems.

☐ Set aside time for students to clean out their desks. You may want to mark it in your lesson plans so you don't forget. Remember to provide this structured time at least once every few weeks or so.

☐ Do occasional supply checks with students. Have them take an inventory of what they have, and then determine what supplies they need to replenish.

☐ Implement a reward system to support students in their efforts to become more organized. Realize the power of specific praise.

13: Student Paperwork

"What the world really
needs is more love and
less paperwork."
— Pearl Bailey

Students have many types of papers to manage. They must keep track of homework-related papers and place these papers where they can easily locate them. They also are responsible for "in-progress" pages, which are worksheets they are currently working on in class. In addition, students must also manage papers to take home (their mail), and they must keep track of the worksheets, notes, or permission slips that they need to return to school. Although it may be difficult to reduce the amount of paperwork, as the chapter quote suggests, teachers can introduce solid systems for helping students organize their papers so students feel in control of the multitude of paperwork they must handle. Given sensible systems and reliable ways to transport papers back and forth, students will have a greater chance for success throughout the school year.

HOMEWORK

In addition to reinforcing the day's lesson, homework teaches students responsibility, time management, the importance of completing a task and how to meet deadlines.

Using a Homework Board and Student Planners

A homework or planner board helps students stay on track with daily homework, long-term projects, and test dates. Setting up this board is simple. Dedicate an area of your dry-erase or chalkboard as the homework area or have a smaller, separate board as the homework area. If you teach multiple subjects, list each subject and then daily update any homework assignments for each subject. If a major project or test is coming up, write a reminder on the homework board, and give guided study instructions if necessary. This board gives students a daily reminder of homework expectations. This visual reminder is a great way to help students clearly understand what homework they need to finish for the next day (or for later in the week).

In order to utilize the homework board effectively, each student needs a planner in which to record his or her assignments.

My school has a standard student planner that the Parent Teacher Organization sells to all students so the format remains the same from year to year. If your school doesn't offer planners, select an affordable, easy-to-find planner, and put it on your supply list so students can purchase it before the start of the year. Help parents by being as specific as possible in the description and let them know where they can purchase the planners. Or have students purchase a separate notebook in which to record homework assignments. At the beginning of the school year, you can also have students staple blank calendar pages into the notebook so they can record important dates throughout the year and see exactly how many days they have to complete a project or study for a test.

When students take the time to record daily assignments, write dates for long-term projects, and include reminders in their planners or calendars for upcoming tests or quizzes, they gain a sense of responsibility and independence. They are enforcing good habits that lead to academic success. Writing down important information related to a due date or deadline is a skill they will continue to use throughout their academic career and into their professional lives. We need to support this habit in our classrooms and insist that students use planners effectively every day.

Here are some tips for using homework boards and planners:

- Ensure that you set aside time each day to update the homework board and allow students to fill out their planners.
- Determine which students, if any, may require a planner check. A student who is chronically late turning in assignments or who regularly doesn't complete his work could benefit from these checks.
- Communicate with parents about your planner checks, and perhaps ask them to initial their child's planner for an additional follow-through to help them turn in work on time.
- Do a planner check for the entire class once or twice per week. I like to check my students' planners once in a while

to ensure that everyone is indeed filling out their planners. In this way, I can keep tabs on students' behaviors and habits in recording their homework. If I notice particular students not filling out their planners, I can talk with those students and also communicate with those students' parents to ask for their support as well.

Methods for Turning in Homework

Each teacher has a different style or preference for how he or she wants students to turn in homework. There is no one best way to perform this task. Simply decide what system works for you, and stick with it so students will always know how to properly turn in work. There are a variety of systems you can use.

Some teachers prefer that students turn in their work in metal or plastic trays in a central location in the classroom. You could label the trays based on the subject area you teach, or if you teach multiple classes in the same subject area, you could organize trays based on a general label like "Period 1," or "Class 2." Some teachers like to use a similar system, only with stacking files instead.

Another idea for turning in work is to use a hanging pocket chart, labeled by class, period, or subject area. Students can turn in homework in manila folders within these pouches. It is a great system to use if space is limited in your classroom. Another method for turning in homework is to use a metal or plastic drawer system. You can label the outside of the drawer based on the subject area or class/period (as in the above examples), and then students simply pull out the drawer and turn in their homework.

Check It Off!

Teachers need a way to ensure that all students have turned in their assignments on the appointed day. Some teachers prefer to do this themselves and take the time to check off students' names on a class spreadsheet. Other teachers ask students to take charge of this task, and ask a selected student to go through the stack of homework papers and check off student names. That student can also be in charge of checking in with the students whose papers are missing, but be sure students do not become bossy in this situation. Discuss ahead of time what dialogue you want them to use when checking in with a student about a missing assignment. Involving students in the accountability process sets a good example. Students see that you are serious about punctuality with homework, and they feel more involved when they actively participate in this task. This strategy for checking for homework completion can work for all levels of students.

Creating a uniform system for students to house all of their papers is one of the most important steps you can take in helping students become (and stay) organized.

Some teachers also utilize a method where students stand up at their seats, and one by one they sit down as the teacher calls out names on papers. Those students who remain standing are the ones who have not turned in work. This method is acceptable and helpful from time to time, but it could lead to students being embarrassed as well. You will need to judge whether or not to implement this strategy.

Whichever method you choose, be sure to have a sensible homework check-in system. It's a good idea to check for homework completion for assignments on the day an assignment is due, or students will sense that they don't need to be prompt with handing in homework.

PAPERS THAT STAY AT SCHOOL

Creating a uniform system for students to house all of their papers is one of the most important steps you can take in helping students become (and stay) organized. It's important to create a system for students to store all of the papers that they are working on in class. These papers are ones that do not require grading, but are not to be sent home. There are a few options for storing these work-in-progress items. You can use a folder system, a subject-area binder, or a portfolio organizer. The first thing to consider is which type of organizer you prefer so you can stay on top of helping students organize this important storage tool properly.

Pocket Organizers

Pocket organizers contain several (usually eight) folders spiral bound with wire or plastic. Another type of pocket organizer is an accordion file, which is expandable and divided into many tabbed sections.

Pros: This type of organizer allows students to store paperwork for a variety of subjects in one place, and the multiple pockets create specific spots for each type of paper. I like to use the bound eight-pocket organizer with my students. I print computer labels and have students place them on the individual pockets of the organizer. The labels look clean and crisp, and they help students remember what type of paper goes in each pocket. Because all of their paperwork is in one place, students rarely forget a worksheet or assignment when they take their materials home.

Cons: If students do not have regular opportunities to purge or clean these organizers, they can become quite bulky. It's a good idea to schedule time at least once every few weeks to clear out old papers or worksheets (see pages 179–180 for ideas on maintaining these organizers). One other con is that the organizer can wear out somewhat quickly if students do not take care of it properly. To prevent this problem, ask students to bring two of these organizers to school at the beginning of the school year. That way, when one of their organizers wears out, they'll have a fresh one available to use.

Binders

Binders come in many sizes, colors, and patterns, and there are many reasons for using them. Tabbed dividers allow students to house papers under many different categories.

Pros: Binders are great for subject-specific paperwork, and tab dividers let you get as specific as you want when organizing a multitude of papers. I have my students use binders to keep their reading paperwork organized in my language arts classes. I ask them to use tab dividers, and I am very specific about how to label each tab. The tabs are set up according to my instructional purposes:

- Reading Lists
- Reading Responses
- Literature Circles and Guided Reading
- Writing
- Word Study

Each of these tabs will hold a variety of paperwork that we will access and use on a daily basis. For example, I have students record their daily reading on a reading log. They also keep a record of books they want to read, as well as a check-off sheet of the genres they are reading to reach their total book goal for the year. All of these pages live under the Reading Lists tab.

Practicality aside, I find there's something special about using a binder for a specific subject or class. I love looking through a student binder at different times of the year; the binder serves as a visual reminder of the things students are experiencing, a record of their adventures in reading, and it becomes a storage hub of their thinking and learning.

Cons: It can take students more time to maintain binders. Students must punch holes in every piece of paper they add. (If you have a photocopier in your building that has a hole-punching function, and you know ahead of time that what you are copying will go into students' binders, you will save yourself a lot of time by using this function.) Binders also tend to take up quite a bit of space, so storage could be an issue. Pages tend to rip out of binders somewhat easily. Invest in some self-adhesive reinforcement holes for papers that accidentally rip out of binders.

Folders

A third option is two-pocket folders with or without brads. For clarity and ease of use, require students to purchase folders that are different colors to keep track of different subject areas. Students may have one folder for math, one for science, another for social studies, and another folder for language arts.

Pros: Separate folders for each subject area help students properly store paperwork so they can easily find what they are looking for. This method is a workable strategy for students, especially in a self-contained classroom where students do not switch classes and where they have easy access to their desk. They can pull out and use these individual folders as needed during the day. If you have a few important papers you want students to house within these folders, opt for the folders with brads. The paperwork is then easily visible and can be referred to when needed.

Cons: Using individual loose folders can contribute to a sense of disorganization. Students may lose individual folders, and these folders can wear out relatively quickly. If students switch rooms multiple times a day, it may be difficult for them to quickly grab what they need when they are looking for more than one folder.

Purging Binders and Folders

At the end of a busy day, we are often happy if we've effectively taught lessons, and we're content if we were able to keep students on task so they completed assignments and behaved appropriately. Teachers rarely have time to think about helping students clean up and organize their materials, but it's vital that we consistently make time to work with students to purge and organize their binders and folders. This structured time is especially important for students in elementary school, but it can still be a positive practice for older students as well. Remember, some students are more naturally inclined to organize their materials, while many others need regular, structured opportunities for purging and clearing out their paper clutter. Here are some general guidelines for clearing out binders and folders:

- Establish categories for the paper: keep at school, take home, and recycle. Set parameters for each category to teach students how to evaluate each piece of paper and put it in the appropriate category. For example, you may tell students to take home any graded assignments they no longer need at school, and you may have them recycle any rough drafts or practice assignments they no longer need.
- Instruct students that when they are unsure whether they can take home or recycle a specific paper, they should ask you about it to help them decide. A good rule of thumb is for them to simply ask you about what to do with specific papers when in doubt.
- Guide students to double check their recycled pile to ensure they don't dispose of any important papers that they need to keep for current units of study.
- Remind students to check their binders and folders regularly (perhaps once every two weeks), and talk with them about becoming more independent in cleaning out their binders/folders/tabbed sections. You could have students write out each of the guidelines for each category of paper and keep these guidelines in their binder so they can sort papers on their own as needed.

Cleaning and purging binders and folders is a great way for students to learn more about organizing and maintaining their paperwork and materials, and it will teach them the positive results of organizing. Keeping only the essentials in their binders and folders will allow them to focus on current content and help them make the most of their study time. Students also will feel a sense of relief and calm when their binders and folders are no longer stuffed to the gills. It keeps the paperwork from becoming overwhelming.

PAPERS THAT GO HOME

Students need to have some sort of folder to take home their mail. Many teachers ask students to use a two-pocket folder dedicated for just this task. One side is for take-home items (for example, graded papers, parent letters, flyers, etc.). The other side is labeled "Return to School" for papers that need to come back to school (for example, signed permission slips, registrations, notes to the teacher, etc.). It may help students and parents if you select a uniform color for this folder (such as red or black) so they can immediately identify the mail folder. If you plan to specify a color, list it on your classroom supply list at the start of the school year.

An effective mail system is crucial in helping students take home graded papers, flyers, announcements, and parent newsletters. You will want to determine a good working system and be consistent about how students carry these documents to and from school on a daily basis.

Use a Mailbox System

Many teachers set up a mail hub where each student has a mailbox that holds his or her mail. This mail includes any graded papers, school flyers, teacher newsletters, and other important mail such as book orders or permission slips. Determine how often you want students to take their mail home. There are a few options:

- **Friday folder.** Hold most of the weekly mail until Friday afternoon so students take the bulk of their mail home on only one day of the week.
- **Daily distribution.** You could have students take their mail home every day so parents can see various forms of communication or graded work more often.

Whichever system you use, be sure that students keep to a schedule and you are consistent with passing out mail. Most teachers designate student helpers to pass out this mail on a regular basis, but you may want to pass out graded tests or quizzes yourself to individual students at their desks during the day so students don't see each others' scores. Taking time to pass out these graded tests in class also gives you the opportunity to review any content as necessary.

Confidential Paperwork
You can still use student mailboxes for confidential papers as long as you make a few provisions. Consider these tips:

- Fold over and then tape or staple any confidential paperwork. Write "To the Parents of…" on the front of the document.
- Consider using a manila envelope and sealing it. Then you can place it into students' mailboxes.
- For time-sensitive or more confidential types of documents, such as an IEP invitation to a parent, your school building or district may have special policies in place that require you to send them through the post office.
- Phone or e-mail parents concerning personal issues. You will reach the parent directly and not have to worry about a handwritten note getting from school to home.

RETURNING PAPERWORK
Determine a system for returning mail back to school. You can request that students simply hand you any paperwork (such as book orders, permission slips, notes from home, etc.) in the morning when they come into the classroom, or you may want to designate a special box, bin, tray, or drawer in which students can place any communication from home. If students hand you the paperwork in the morning, be sure to sort it daily and process or file it as needed. Designate a spot on your desk to place unsorted correspondence so it doesn't get overlooked or misplaced with other papers. This spot could be your own mailbox within the room.

Tips for Organizing Student Papers

☐ Use a homework/planner board each day. Set up clear systems for filling out this board. Insist students use planners, and do regular planner checks to ensure students are properly filing out their planners.

☐ Determine how you want students to turn in homework. Consider various trays, files, or drawers. Initiate a system for checking off homework, either on your own or by enlisting student assistance on the day it is due.

☐ Decide on the type of storage system you want students to use to house paperwork. Use proper labels, and use these systems regularly.

☐ Provide set times to clean out or purge binders or folders. Walk students through the process, and give them clear categories for clearing out their paper clutter. Use simple designations of keep at school, take home, or recycle.

☐ Determine appropriate systems for sending papers home and returning paperwork to school.

14: The End of the Year

"We are what we repeatedly do. Excellence, then, is not an act but a habit."
— Aristotle

The final days of the school year are near! You've been working your way toward finalizing grade cards, organizing and filing end-of-year documents, and thinking about organizing your room for the summer. Things tend to become overwhelming at the end of the school year, and your classroom organizing efforts can really suffer due to the hectic pace and stress level of this time period. If you take time to plan efficiently and think carefully about what needs to be done to end the year well, you can eliminate—or at least greatly reduce—the stress of year-end procedures.

> Take time to plan efficiently and think carefully about what needs to be done to end the year well to eliminate the stress of year-end procedures.

IDENTIFY KEY AREAS OF NEED

As the end of the year approaches, several areas in my classroom need attention. No matter how well I've worked with students to keep the classroom well ordered, I will need to take steps to tweak or reorganize certain spaces. For instance, my classroom library is very well organized. Books are clearly labeled by genre, and students are able to maintain the library well throughout the school year. But inevitably, as students are rushed to turn in books or use less care as the year progresses, I notice that several books are out of place and the bins are a bit messy.

Think about the areas within your classroom that are messy, disorganized, or dirty. These are probably high-use or high-traffic areas as well as areas that you left under the care of students. Identify exactly what needs to be done so when you leave for the summer, you have a specific plan to ready your classroom for the next groups of students when you return in the fall.

Enlist Student Help

After you've identified your problem areas, create a plan for reorganizing them. One of the best ways to ensure that your classroom is well maintained at the end of the school year is to provide opportunities for students to help you clean and organize. Recently, I created an end-of-the-year classroom job board with descriptions of tasks and spaces for students to sign up for tasks that they would like to perform. I made these tasks optional but found that students were

Ideas for Student Helpers

Providing students with an opportunity to help clean and organize at the end of the year is one of the best ways to maintain your classroom. Here are some ideas for jobs you can ask students to volunteer to perform. Remember that these are optional/suggested tasks (your school or district may have guidelines regarding students helping with organizing the classroom at the end of the school year).

- Library Helpers: Organize all library books; sort and organize neatly in bins. Dust shelves and place bins back on shelves.

- Recess Games: Pull out all recess games. Identify any missing pieces; put back in appropriate game boxes. Organize games carefully within drawers.

- Lockers and Cubby Area: Pull everything out of the locker and cubby area. Use cleaning wipes to dust and clean all surfaces.

- Computer Tables: Use cleaning wipes to clean computer tables and keyboards. Use special dusting cloths to dust computer monitors.

- Shelving Units (Borrow Boxes/Student Supplies): Use cleaning wipes to clean the classroom "borrow boxes" shelving unit. Take off all borrow boxes, and clean each shelf. Allow to dry before replacing the boxes on the shelf.

very eager to help organize and clean the classroom. Doing so gives them a sense of accomplishment; in addition, students are usually very willing to please their teachers. See the sidebar on page 186 for ideas of end-of-year class jobs.

Be Realistic

Although students (especially in upper grades) can take charge of a large number of projects, you still must oversee student work and be willing to take extra steps to finish anything that may not have been completed to your satisfaction. It's important to expect this, but don't let this expectation deter you from letting students help. Students gain a deeper sense of responsibility and pride when they are asked to take care of a given space. If your students had some ownership in setting up and maintaining order in various spaces in the classroom during the course of the year, helping to organize and clean them at the end of the year should seem like a natural progression to the students. Still, you may need to complete a variety of tasks on your own after the students' last day of school.

Many teachers complete last-minute tasks on a teacher work-day following the students' last day. An important last-minute task is to finish filing any paperwork, including residual papers for curricular units. Each year, I typically have quite a pile left to file, and in the midst of the busy end-of-year schedule, it's easy to forget to take time to file these papers. However, it's an important step because you don't want to lose or misplace these papers and risk not being able to access them in a timely manner during the next school year.

REORGANIZING YOUR MATERIALS

The easiest way to leave your room clearly organized at the end of the year is to evaluate and reorganize your materials in each class-room zone. (Review organizing ideas for classroom zones in Chapter 5.) As you evaluate each zone consider the following:

Question: What materials or supplies need to be rearranged, organized, or stored elsewhere in preparation for the end of the school year?

Suggestions: Working within one zone at a time, determine if you have supplies that need to be sorted or rearranged. Decide whether you need to organize your materials more thoroughly or perhaps in a different way. What level of organizing works for you? Can you easily find things when they are separated in large, distinct categories (such as by subject), or do you want even more distinction within the categories? For instance, you may need to store supplies for a specific science unit in a few clear plastic boxes, or you might find that you have specific materials for a social studies unit that can be labeled and stored more appropriately. However, you may be fine having one bin for all science materials and another for all social studies items.

Organize to a level that lets you easily find what you are looking for while still allowing for easy maintenance. If you are not a meticulous or detailed person, don't set up a meticulous or detailed system—it will frustrate you, which will cause you not to use the system. Clearly label everything so you can identify the container you are seeking with only a glance.

Next, think about whether you can store items elsewhere. If you do need certain supplies or materials but have another suitable storage area for them (especially if they are common supplies that more than one teacher may use at your grade level), take them to that storage area, and put them away neatly. Completing this task is productive and helpful in two ways. First, you have cleared some space for yourself in the classroom by taking some supplies to another location, and second, you have properly replaced items that are common to other teachers.

Question: What do you need to purge from each zone of your classroom? (See Chapter 3 for specific information and tips about purging.)

Suggestions: Are there items you didn't use this year—and you know you won't use next year, either? If you don't need or plan to use various items, donate them to another teacher or grade level. This decreases the clutter in your classroom, and you can be sure that what you are keeping is truly useful. If you purge in smaller spurts through the school year, this purging process shouldn't feel too overwhelming because you will simply be skimming off the most recent layer of clutter from your materials and supplies. If you haven't been able to purge in stages during the current school year, the purging process will probably take longer. Though tedious, the purging stage is important. Thoughtfully purge and organize each classroom zone. The more you do now, the less you'll have to do later!

> Though tedious, the purging stage is very important. Thoughtfully purge and organize each classroom zone. The more you do now, the less you'll have to do later!

Question: Do you need to replenish any supplies or materials?

Suggestions: Create a list of supplies you need to buy, either for student use or personal use. Use the Supplies Inventory Checklist on page 208 in the appendix to help you determine supplies you need to order. Taking inventory at the end of the year means you don't need to take inventory at the start of the year. You'll also efficiently use the items you have on hand, and you won't find yourself with too few or too many supplies.

Find a convenient space to store any new supplies that you buy for the upcoming school year. When I replenish my paper clips, pens, pencils, tape, staples, or other general teacher supplies, I house them in the same two drawers in my teacher cabinet so I always know where to find them.

PLAN AND ORGANIZE YOUR SUMMER STORAGE

Each building and school district will have guidelines for how teachers are to leave their classrooms at the end of the year. You may need to empty all moveable furniture (including your teacher desk, carts, and bookcases) so the custodial staff can move it to thoroughly clean and maintain the floors. Determine what you need to do to fulfill these guidelines first. Then use your energy and creativity to make smart organizational decisions about how to leave your classroom so when you enter your room in late summer to get it ready for a new school year, you'll feel calm rather than overwhelmed.

Surface Items

Regardless of whether your furniture will be moved during the summer, it's logical to clear surface items from your desk and the tops of shelving units. Remove pictures, stuffed animals, knickknacks, or personal items. Take any personal or treasured items home, and store them there until the new school year begins. If you feel comfortable keeping these items at school, place them in a labeled container and find an appropriate storage area. (Don't feel obligated to buy a container; you can use any cardboard box.) Don't store surface items in your desk drawers if the furniture will be moved. The drawers could slide open and items could spill out.

Temporary Storage

If you need to move large quantities of materials (binders, teacher resources, chapter books, etc.) off of your moveable furniture, have a plan in place, rather than haphazardly placing materials around the classroom. Determine the best storage area for these items, and think about how best to place them. Here are some options and tips for using these areas:

- **Locker or cubby area.** Stack material in the same order it appears in its permanent home. Use a different locker or cubby for each shelf. Label the locker with the corresponding shelf (for example, third shelf bookcase or second shelf cabinet) so you can quickly replace the items at the start of the year.

- **Open shelves in your room.** Again, keep things in order and label them.
- **Countertops.** Make the most of this space by using containers. Use a separate container for each shelf you are clearing, and label each container. You don't need to purchase containers. You can use cardboard boxes from the cafeteria or shoeboxes for smaller desk items.

Protecting Materials

You many need to cover materials or move them to different places within your classroom in the summer months to prevent things from becoming too dirty or dusty. First, find out if your school has specific guidelines for storing or covering items in your classroom. Then, work within those guidelines to find the best method of protecting your materials. Some options include covering bookshelves or open storage areas, such as locker or cubbies, with large sections of butcher paper. (I still clean these areas as I am setting up my room before the school year begins, but I like having these areas covered during the summer, nonetheless).

Take time to properly clean your computer screens and keyboards, and cover them so they are protected during the summer months.

DETERMINING PROFESSIONAL GOALS

So, you've decided how to store various supplies. You've determined a plan for organizing your materials so you can access them as soon as you need them at the beginning of the new school year. What else do you need to consider as you prepare for the year ahead? The end of the current school year may seem a bit premature to think about what you want to change or improve upon in your instruction for the coming year, but we are most aware of what we have accomplished and what we need to improve at the end of the year. Our instruction is still fresh in our minds, and we have a good idea of where we were able to shine in our teaching and where we need to grow as an educator. I typically find myself in a more reflective mood at this time of the school year, and perhaps you do, too. What better time to think about our goals for next year?

Professional reflections are very valuable. They can guide you toward good instructional decisions and help you focus on professional development and summer reading opportunities.

There are many different measures we can study to determine areas of strength and weakness (such as end-of-year assessments in various subjects, student observations and surveys, as well as standardized tests), but we can get an early feel for our goals for the next year by reflecting on the previous year and giving a bit of thought to the upcoming year. Professional reflections are very valuable. They can guide you toward good instructional decisions and help you focus on professional development and summer reading opportunities. Consider the following steps as you think about your professional goals:

Identify Areas of Strength

It's always a good idea to start the goal-setting process with a positive frame of mind. Identify aspects of your instruction about which you feel confident. Identify one or two specific things you implemented, changed, improved upon, or continued from last year that helped to enrich students' learning experiences during the school year. Be specific. Identifying these affirmative instructional practices or procedures helps to internalize positive feelings about your hard work and efforts. For example, last year I made some changes to how I implemented independent reading with my students. I made a stronger commitment to conferencing with my students, working hard to communicate and educate them to set monthly goals for their reading. I observed that taking time to conference with them increased their appreciation for the reading process (which was one of my main goals for students), so this was a very positive aspect of growth for me. I continue to work on how I can use aspects of conferencing with students in reading to help them set and reach their goals in tangible ways.

Determine Areas for Improvement

Now that you have identified some positive aspects of your teaching, you can think about what changes you want to make for the upcoming year. It's important to realize that any professional modifications you make in your instruction do not need to be wide, sweeping changes. Rather, you may decide to change a small part of instruction so something runs more smoothly or so some aspect of instruction is made clearer. For instance, in my reading workshop, I usually feel confident with the fiction titles I use during various aspects of my reading instruction, but I felt I needed to work on incorporating a wider variety of nonfiction in my classroom instruction. I reflected about how much nonfiction I personally read in my own life and how it can play such an amazing role in helping me learn and grow. Students need this same kind of exposure from an early age to guide them in learning about a range of topics and subjects. So it only made sense for me to strive toward a goal of initiating more nonfiction in my teaching lessons. This is important not only to fulfill various grade-level objectives or standards in my lessons, but also because it promotes variety in student reading choices.

This is just one example of how to reflect about a certain aspect of your teaching, but my aim was to share the process of identifying an area of need and then determining a specific area for growth.

Evaluate Current Units

When you decide upon a specific area of improvement, think about your current units of study. Sometimes when you want to make a change in your instructional practice, you can make some of these changes within the existing units rather than as add-ons to your instruction. This is particularly important because we cannot continually add more tasks to our instruction without taking something away. Determine what activities you currently incorporate within your instruction. Think about the purpose of the units you teach. Then think of what you may want to do differently with your instruction. Is it a different teaching approach? Specific activities you want to try in place of others? Do you want to try a different approach with classroom discipline, or

> Whatever your goal, determine ways to weave various changes into your current instruction so you are not creating extra work for yourself.

End-of-Year Checklist

☐ Identify key areas of need by determining which areas in your room are the most disorganized. Think in terms of your classroom zones to help you in this process.

☐ Enlist student help in organizing your classroom at the end of the year.

☐ Be realistic in your expectation of student helpers. They will likely need a lot of support and structure. Acknowledge that you may need to help with tasks in order to complete them to your satisfaction.

☐ Finish any filing you haven't gotten to during the school year so you don't lose important papers over the summer.

☐ Take time to purge supplies and materials. Clearing clutter will ensure that you are keeping only what you need and use.

☐ Replenish supplies you need for the upcoming year. Keep track of supplies you need by referencing the Supplies Inventory Checklist on page 208 in the appendix.

incorporate a new classroom procedure, such as classroom meetings or a reward system? Whatever your goal, determine ways to weave various changes into your current instruction so you are not creating extra work for yourself. We want our teaching strategies to do as much as possible in order to present students with as many learning opportunities as we can so they receive a well-rounded education, but we can't do it all. More isn't always better. It's important to remember to emphasize quality over quantity (more about this in Chapter 15). You can use the Professional Goals Self-Evaluation sheet on page 221 in the appendix to help with goal setting.

- ☐ Consider reasonable and efficient procedures for storing surface items.
- ☐ Properly store your materials and supplies. For each zone of your classroom, determine what materials or supplies need to be rearranged, organized, or stored elsewhere prior to the end of the school year. Remember to label, label, label!
- ☐ Take time to thoughtfully evaluate your strengths from the previous school year.
- ☐ Identify areas for professional growth for the next year. Consider doing some summer reading and professional development during your break.
- ☐ Incorporate activities or changes in curriculum within your current units, when appropriate, to maximize productivity without producing a sense of overload.

15: It's All About Balance

"Balance, peace, and joy are the fruit of a successful life. It starts with recognizing your talents and finding ways to serve others by using them."

— Thomas Kinkade

What is the key to keeping it together as a teacher? What do we need to do to keep from burning out? How do we remain encouraged and enthused about our profession when pressures continue to mount each year? How can we find time to recharge our batteries during the busy, consuming school year? The answer to all of these questions is balance. We must learn how to balance our time and our obligations, our stress and our leisure, our expectations and our realities. This chapter will help you find balance in a few key areas that are often problematic for teachers.

QUALITY, NOT QUANTITY

Although this phrase is a bit of a cliché, I have determined that one of the keys to becoming a truly effective teacher is to embrace this belief wholeheartedly. There was a time in my teaching when I thought that the more items I crossed off of a list of things to do with students, the better. I tried to cram as much into my day as possible, even though I wasn't really considering that the quality in these activities might have been lacking. Days during this time felt rushed, and by lunchtime, I was thoroughly exhausted. Although I am generally still tired by lunchtime, I have revised my thinking in the past several years.

Expectations are high for teachers on many levels, but I know that I have to set reasonable and meaningful expectations for my daily life with students. I must be thoughtful and purposeful about every single thing I do with my students each day. There will surely be times when I won't be 100 percent prepared for my day, but to the extent that I can, I need to carefully consider my time with students so the aspect of quality is never sacrificed. The quantity may be reduced to an extent, which does sometimes feel wrong, but it most definitely is not wrong to maintain high standards for the quality we put into our teaching. In fact, it's empowering and fulfilling. We may feel frustrated if we don't get a few tasks checked off in our daily plans because we'll need to move some tasks a day forward in our weekly lesson plans, but addressing quality in our teaching never ignores the value of the activities we do with our students.

I also like to think of aspects of "quality, not quantity" in relation to everyday life. I want my life experience to truly be about quality. Though quantity is also nice, I usually feel as if I want to spend more quality time with others; I don't think in terms of quantity of time as a major factor in determining happiness or success. Whether you are a first-year teacher or a thirty-year veteran, reinforce and appreciate this distinction to effectively prioritize and manage your time.

ONE DAY AT A TIME

If you are like me, it is difficult to deal with not having everything checked off of your daily to-do list. It's not easy to have an ongoing to-grade pile in my teacher bag. It's hard for me to accept that my files are not perfect, and it's uncomfortable knowing I have some tasks left undone, just waiting for me the next day. I would much rather complete all of these things before leaving school. Several years ago, after making a change in my teaching assignment, I often would work ten-hour days. Walking out to the parking lot at 6:30 or 7 P.M., I noticed that my car was often the last one there. I was driving myself to a point of near exhaustion to finish tasks. I had certainly not learned that it was going to be essential for me to take things one day at a time in my teaching career. It was a hard lesson to learn because I was letting my type-A personality cause me to refuse anything less than perfect.

Certainly, you will have those days when you will need to stay late, and it's important to schedule time appropriately for those occasions. But I quickly learned that taking this approach on a consistent basis caused me much more strife and less enthusiasm toward teaching in the long run. Though I still work late from time to time (like everyone else in the working world!), I've been much better about managing my time and understanding that it is okay to leave some tasks for the morrow. Nothing is so important that it cannot wait until the next day. I know now that if something really is very pressing on my calendar or on my to-do list, I can make it a top priority for the next day.

STRESS MANAGEMENT

There are many books on stress management, and many of the tips and suggestions within these books are extremely helpful for promoting a healthier life. As teachers, we have to be vigilant about taking measures to reduce the stress in our lives to ensure that we do our job efficiently. We need to stay healthy and motivated, or we risk possible exhaustion, burnout, or illness. Truth be told, I have not done as well as I would like with managing aspects of stress at work. Part of this is due to my personality; I tend to bring some of the stress on myself. But the other reality is that teachers are so busy now—more than ever—and our stress levels are increasing in tandem. I know that I am more stressed now than I was as a beginning teacher. How do we manage these stress levels so we can come to work and still appreciate and enjoy our jobs?

Self-Care

There are many ways to promote self-care. Each teacher has different ways to recharge and rejuvenate. With other responsibilities in life, whether children, other jobs, housework, laundry, and more, it's not always easy to determine how to find time and fit in dedicated moments of self-care. I contend that taking care of yourself as a teacher is more important than ever before so we can reach out to others and continue to perform well as an educator.

Self-care is not about pampering as much as it is about intentionally scheduling ways in which you can promote a sense of calm. Self-care is about doing things purposefully in order to come back to center and feel whole again. Determine what you love to do to help you relax, and find time to do these things. I tend to agree with experts who suggest that you should even put activities for downtime on your calendar so you really do make it a top priority. Scheduling time for yourself is critical to keeping a positive outlook and promoting balance. Decide if you might want to do any of the following:

- Exercise
- Read
- Talk to a friend (on the phone, on social networks, etc.)
- Write a letter or e-mail to a friend or relative
- Go shopping
- Take a bubble bath or long shower
- Pray
- Do some deep breathing
- Play a game with your spouse or children
- Take a walk (alone, with a loved one, or with your dog if you have one)
- Sit outside and enjoy some time appreciating nature
- Get a massage
- Plan a picnic with your family
- Visit relatives
- Write in a journal
- Take a nap
- Watch television
- Take time for a hobby you love

These are a few of the many possible activities in which you can participate to recharge your batteries and give yourself much needed "you" time. As the quote says at the beginning of this chapter, we must find a true sense of balance, peace, and joy in order to feel truly fulfilled in our teaching lives and beyond.

Monitoring Your Life

When things get hectic and you don't know how you can fit any more into your existing day, you need to take time to consider how to make lasting change in your life. Sometimes this may mean radical changes, such as taking a year off from teaching or changing your schedule significantly so you can gain a better sense of calm in life.

Or it may mean making numerous, smaller changes that add up to meaningful, lasting change. When times get rough, we tend to think that we can hack it because we always seem to find a way to work through obstacles at school when we need to. But it is never a good idea to take on so many things or become so stressed that you no longer enjoy teaching or feel as if you can't do any more. Realize that understanding your boundaries is not a sign of weakness, but rather a sign of strength. Give yourself permission to discover what you need to do to maintain perspective and still appreciate the work you do. Acknowledge that you are important and that self-care is an essential part of improving your life. Then you can feel confident about putting forth your best effort in the classroom each day.

> Realize that understanding your boundaries is not a sign of weakness, but rather a sign of strength. Give yourself permission to discover what you need to do to maintain perspective and still appreciate the work you do.

Calendars and More

It is essential to keep your calendar organized and up-to-date. Does it seem as if you have more and more meetings each year? You need to be able to keep track of all of your commitments. Whether you use a paper calendar or you keep track of appointments and meetings via an electronic device, be diligent about entering all of the information you need in order to stay on top of your responsibilities. (This includes self-care appointments for yourself, too!) Because you may have other family commitments, such as transporting your own children to practices, games, or other appointments, you must be a master manager of your own calendar. Be diligent about entering information on your calendar, and make it a habit to look carefully at the upcoming week's scheduled events. Make note of any changes in your daily appointments, and keep up-to-date on your personal engagements as well, such as doctor or dentist appointments, hair appointments, or other outside activities.

Don't Spread Yourself Too Thin

When you feel harried and rushed all of the time, going from one meeting to another and one activity to the next, think carefully about your commitments. Are you over-involved? Have you signed up for too many committees at school? It's certainly important to be an active participant in your building. Being involved helps you feel connected and promotes a sense of teamwork with staff members. Taking the initiative to become involved in a building committee or two gives you perspective and helps you learn and grow in many ways. Being on committees also helps you develop yourself professionally. Think about where you feel you can offer some aspect of leadership. You likely have much to offer in the way of professional contributions to a variety of groups. However, some teachers may get too involved and push themselves too far, signing up for four or five committees (or more!). They attend meetings constantly, and therefore do not have time to maintain aspects of their teaching as well as they'd like. In the end, you'll feel more content knowing you are making meaningful contributions in a few specific areas, rather than feeling as if you can barely keep up. It goes back to "quality, not quantity."

Balance, Balance, Balance!

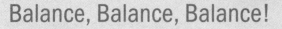

☐ Think about the phrase "quality, not quantity." Initiate practices within your instruction that promote depth of learning for your students, not just in how much you teach them.

☐ Make small changes to your schedule and your teaching practices to help you take things one day at a time. Make it a habit to prioritize carefully, and learn to be okay with having things on your to-do list for the next day. Remember, whatever you don't get done today will still be there tomorrow.

☐ Identify activities that will help you to recharge and reenergize. Identify at least four or five things you enjoying doing and that will help you to relax after a long day.

☐ Be an excellent manager of your calendar. Enter all appointments, and keep track of any changes. Be sure to enter self-care activities so you see them as commitments to yourself, not just leisure activities.

☐ Be thoughtful about your involvement in committees and other activities at school. Sign up and become involved in school committees regarding topics or subjects about which you are passionate, but refrain from joining too many committees or participating in too many activities.

SUGGESTED READING LIST

Organizing Your Classroom Library/Reading Resources

Getting Started: The Reading-Writing Workshop, Grades 4–8 by Linda Ellis and Jamie Marsh (Heinemann)

Guiding Readers and Writers, Grades 3–6: Teaching Comprehension, Genre, and Content Literacy by Irene C. Fountas and Gay Su Pinnell (Heinemann)

Spaces & Places: Designing Classrooms for Literacy by Debbie Diller (Stenhouse Publishers)

The Book Whisperer: Awakening the Inner Reader in Every Child by Donalyn Miller (Jossey-Bass)

Technology Resources

Blogs, Wikis, Podcasts, and Other Powerful Web Tools for Classrooms by Will Richardson (Corwin Press)

Blogs, Wikis, and Podcasts, Oh My!: Electronic Media in the Classroom by Jeffrey Piontek and Blane Conklin (Shell Education)

Children and Organizing

The Organized Student by Donna Goldberg (with Jennifer Zwiebel) (Fireside)

Organizing From the Inside Out for Teenagers by Julie Morgenstern and Jessi Morgenstern-Colon (Henry Holt & Company, LLC)

Where's My Stuff? The Ultimate Teen Organizing Guide by Samantha Moss (Zest Books)

Time Management

Simplify Your Time: Stop Running & Start Living! by Marcia Ramsland (Thomas Nelson)

Time Management From the Inside Out by Julie Morgenstern (Henry Holt & Company, LLC)

General Books on Organizing

Organizing Plain & Simple by Donna Smallin (Storey Publishing)

It's All Too Much: An Easy Plan for Living a Richer Life With Less Stuff by Peter Walsh (Free Press)

One Thing at a Time: 100 Simple Ways to Live Clutter-Free Every Day by Cindy Glovinsky (St. Martin's Griffin)

TOUR OF YOUR ROOM PLANNING SHEET (CHAPTER 2)

Student Desks

Are more desks needed? _____ How many? _____

Do heights need to be adjusted? _____ Mark those desks.

How will you configure the desks? Draw a diagram if this is easier.

_____

_____

_____

Student Materials

Inventory your materials and note the quantity you need for each:

_____	Rulers	_____	Glue	_____	Pens
_____	Pencils	_____	Markers	_____	Notebooks
_____	Crayons	_____	Calculators	_____	Construction paper
_____	Other	_____	Other	_____	Other

How will you store these materials? _____

Classroom Library/Resources

Is the current setup effective? _____

What do you like about the system? _____

_____

What don't you like? _____

What do you want to change? _____

_____

Other Classroom Spaces

Jot down your thoughts about these areas:

Computer area: _____

Recess/game area: _____

Teacher reference shelf: _____

Filing cabinets: _____

FURNITURE CONSIDERATIONS PLANNING SHEET (CHAPTER 2)

This planning sheet will help you identify what you want to include in your classroom to make it organized, warm, and inviting.

Step 1: Record any district or building rules about bringing in various furniture pieces, accessories, or other items.

_____

_____

_____

_____

Step 2: Identify furniture items or accessories you would like to incorporate into your room. Mark those you want to include:

_____ Pillows	_____ Bean bags	_____ Wall decorations
_____ Plants	_____ Area rug(s)	_____ Lamps (desk or floor)
_____ Chairs	_____ Small couch or loveseat	

_____ Other_____

_____ Other_____

Step 3: Draw a diagram of how you want to arrange your room, and specify where you will place each piece of furniture or accessory.

ASSESSING CLASSROOM SPACES SHEET (CHAPTER 3)

Answer the following questions about specific areas in your classroom. Spaces
to consider are: teacher cabinets, teacher shelves (for resources and manuals),
classroom library or resource shelves, recess games area, and any other specific
area you have in your room. Use these answers and the information in chapter 3 to
help you decide what to purge and what to keep. Be as specific as possible.

What do you like about how you have organized this space?

_____

_____

What do you dislike? _____

_____

_____

How can you improve the things you dislike? _____

_____

_____

Look through the area (opening doors and drawers if needed).
What items need to be moved to a different area of the room (write the new location next to the item)? _____

_____

_____

_____

_____

What items need to be recycled, donated, or trashed? _____

_____

_____

_____

_____

_____

SUPPLIES INVENTORY CHECKLIST (CHAPTER 3)

Just as students need to buy new school supplies each year, teachers need to keep track of their supply needs. Start with the following ideas, and add your own ideas as needed on this list.

_____ Ballpoint pens

_____ Binder clips

_____ Chart paper

_____ Clear tape refills

_____ Construction paper

_____ Correction fluid

_____ Dry-erase markers

_____ Fine-point permanent markers

_____ Masking tape

_____ Overhead pens

_____ Paper clips

_____ Staples

_____ Sticky notes (variety of sizes)

_____ Other_____

_____ Other_____

_____ Other_____

_____ Other_____

_____ Other_____

_____ Other_____

_____ Other_____

IMPORTANT STUDENT MEDICAL INFORMATION (CHAPTER 6)

School Year _____

CONFIDENTIAL

Allergy Information

Student Name   Allergy

1. _____   _____
2. _____   _____
3. _____   _____
4. _____   _____
5. _____   _____
6. _____   _____
7. _____   _____

Student Medications

Student Name   Name of Medication

1. _____   _____
2. _____   _____
3. _____   _____
4. _____   _____
5. _____   _____
6. _____   _____
7. _____   _____

Other Student Conditions (Seizures, Diabetes, etc.)

Student Name   Name of Condition

1. _____   _____
2. _____   _____
3. _____   _____
4. _____   _____
5. _____   _____
6. _____   _____
7. _____   _____

STUDENT INVENTORY SHEET (CHAPTER 7)

Date _____

Student name _____

1. How are you feeling about school right now?

_____

_____

2. Tell me one or two of your strengths as a learner.

_____

_____

3. What do you struggle with the most in school?

_____

_____

4. What is the most important thing I can do to help you this year?

_____

_____

5. Is there anything about the classroom or class procedures that I need to explain more about?

_____

_____

6. Are you feeling good about the school year so far?

_____

_____

7. What questions do you have for me?

_____

_____

PARENT CONTACT FORM (CHAPTER 7)

School year _____

Student name _____

KEY:
TC = Telephone Contact
EM = E-mail Contact
PTN = Parent/Teacher Note
PTC = Parent/Teacher Conference

Date	Code	Comments

YEARLY CURRICULUM MAP, BLANK (CHAPTER 9)

Subject	August	September	October	November	December

School year: _____

January	February	March	April	May	Subject

YEARLY CURRICULUM MAP, COMPLETED EXAMPLE (CHAPTER 9)

Subject	August	September	October	November	December
Language Arts	What is Reading/Writing Workshop? Independent reading Writing "seeds" in journals	Reading assessments Reading conferences/goals Writing a narrative piece	Reading Workshop Focus: Strategies Writing Workshop: Narrative piece & begin mystery writing	Reading Workshop: Guided reading Writing Workshop: Finish mystery writing Revising and editing mini lessons	Reading Workshop: Individual conferences/guided reading Writing Workshop: Poetry writing
Math	Numeration Adding and subtracting whole numbers and decimals	Multiplying whole numbers Dividing with 1-digit divisors	Dividing with 2-digit divisors Variables and expressions	Multiplying and dividing decimals Shapes/geometry	Fractions and decimals Adding and subtracting fractions and mixed numbers
Science	Ways of knowing Scientific Method	Physical science	Physical science	Earth science	Earth science
Social Studies	Geography of the United States	Regions of the United States	Native Americans cultural regions	The New World Routes of exploration	English settlements, early colonies
Other					

School year: _____

January	February	March	April	May	Subject
Reading Workshop: Reviewing reading strategies	Reading Workshop: Literature circles/guided reading	Reading Workshop: Finish lit circles, start book clubs	Reading Workshop: Finish book clubs, evaluate goals	Reading Workshop: Strategy review, planning for summer	**Language Arts**
Writing Workshop: Persuasive writing	Writing Workshop: Persuasive writing	Writing Workshop: Research	Writing Workshop: Research	Writing Workshop: Presentations	
Multiplying fractions and mixed numbers Perimeter and area	Solids Measurement units, time, and temperature	Ratio/percent Equations and graphs Solving and writing equations and inequalities	Graphs and data Transformations, congruence, and symmetry	Probability	**Math**
Life science	Life science	Research	Research	Presentations and final projects	**Science**
Slavery	Declaration of Independence, Revolutionary War	Revolutionary War, Constitution	The Bill of Rights, Manifest Destiny	Settling the West	**Social Studies**
					Other

SUBSTITUTE FEEDBACK FORM (CHAPTER 9)

To the Substitute: Use this form to tell me about your experience in our classroom today or, if you prefer, write your own note. I strongly believe in the importance of communication between the regular teacher and substitute teacher. Thanks again for coming in today!

Name of substitute teacher: _____

Date: _____

May I call or e-mail you?_____

Phone number: _____

E-mail address: _____

General comments about the day:

_____

_____

_____

_____

_____

Concerns or questions (include problems/praises):

_____

_____

_____

_____

_____

What things can I explain more clearly for substitute teachers in the future?

_____

_____

_____

_____

_____

PARENT QUESTIONNAIRE (CHAPTER 10)

Family Information

Student's full name: _____

Name your child prefers: _____

Parents' first and last names: _____

Street address: _____ City_____ Zip _____

E-mail addresses: _____

    (I will use e-mail for lots of communication, so please list all e-mail address-
es you'd like me to include in my e-mail address book for these communications—e.g., work/home)

Best phone number to reach you: _____

What is the most effective way for me to communicate with you? (Please circle)
By phone   By e-mail

Please circle the following things your child has access to at home:
Computer Internet E-mail Printer

Child's birthday: _____

Siblings and ages: _____

Pets: _____

How does your child get to school?   Walk   Car   Bus (Please circle)

Who does the student live with? (Circle all that apply)
Mother   Father   Stepmother   Stepfather   Grandparent(s)   Aunt   Uncle

Background information regarding religious background and/or holidays celebrated (or not celebrated). _____

_____

Does your child wear glasses?_____ For (circle)   Reading   Board work   Both

List any medical/physical conditions and food/medicine allergies.

_____

_____

PARENT QUESTIONNAIRE (CHAPTER 10)

Academic Information

1. Describe your child's talents and skills (e.g., dance, art, sports, music).

_____

_____

2. What are some of the things that may impact your child's learning (e.g. extrovert/introvert, expressive, organized/unorganized, listening, health issues)?

_____

_____

3. How does your child spend his/her free time (e.g., read, play outside, TV)?

_____

_____

4. What do you do to motivate your child (e.g., family activity, positive feedback)?

_____

_____

5. How does your child solve problems (e.g., risks, tentative, impulsive, avoids)?

_____

_____

6. Where, when and how does your child do his/her homework and study (e.g., quiet place, common area, quiet music playing)?

_____

_____

7. What can I do help your child become a more efficient learner?

_____

_____

8. Is there something about your child you can share to help me develop a rapport with him/her (e.g., special event, important pet, friend, relative)?

_____

_____

Student Questionnaire

Please fill out the following student questionnaire with your child if possible; if not, please complete it from your point of view.

1. Which things do you do well (e.g. understand people, problem solve, math, sports, sing)?

_____

_____

2. What would you like to be able to do better?

_____

_____

3. How do you learn best (alone, groups, from books, discussions, hands-on)?

_____

_____

4. What do you like best about school?

_____

_____

5. What do you like least about school?

_____

_____

6. Who are the most important people in your life? Why?

_____

_____

7. What kind of work do you want to do when you grow up?

_____

_____

Please add any other comments at the bottom/on the back of this paper. Thank you so much for taking the time to fill this out. This information will be very helpful as I get to know your child.

Created by Judi Chlebus; modified by Melanie Unger.

GENERAL WEEKLY SCHEDULE (CHAPTER 11)

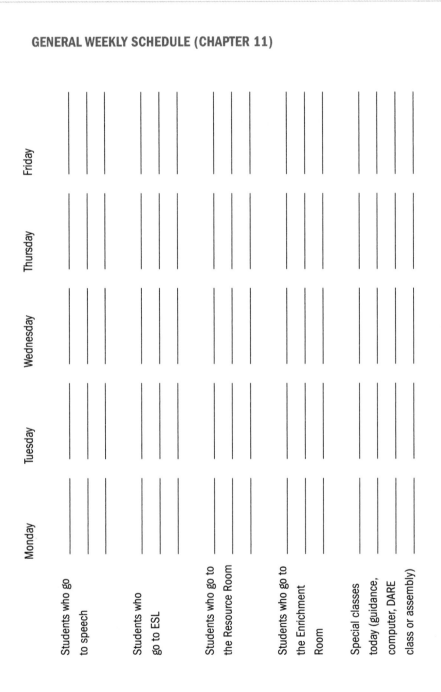

	Monday	Tuesday	Wednesday	Thursday	Friday
Students who go to speech					
Students who go to ESL					
Students who go to the Resource Room					
Students who go to the Enrichment Room					
Special classes today (guidance, computer, DARE class or assembly)					

PROFESSIONAL GOALS SELF-EVALUATION (CHAPTER 14)

Areas of Strength
What am I doing well in my classroom professionally? (Reflect on units of study, classroom activities, classroom atmosphere, classroom discipline, parent communication, incorporating technology.)

1. _____

2. _____

3. _____

Areas for Professional Growth
What do I want to change or improve professionally? (Reflect on things that didn't run efficiently or smoothly, or areas of curriculum that were lacking in depth or scope, for example.)

1. _____

2. _____

3. _____

Action Steps
What realistic and purposeful changes do I want to initiate? (Reflect on possible teaching methods or activities, a different approach with classroom discipline, or a new classroom procedure.)

1. _____

2. _____

3. _____

Index

Books of Interest

Home-Ec 101
by Heather Solos
Whether it's cleaning grout, stocking a pantry, reducing a recipe, dealing with chocolate in the carpet or retrieving jewelry dropped down the drain, *Home-Ec 101* will help you feel confident in managing the domestic challenges of everyday life. Hundreds of helpful tips cover everything you need to know to keep your home clean and in good repair.

Organize Now!
by Jennifer Ford Berry
Get practical, action-oriented organizing advice that you can use to organize any part of your life in less that one week. Quick, easy-to-follow checklists let you spend more time organizing and less time reading—a perfect fit for your busy lifestyle.

Organized Simplicity
by Tsh Oxenreider
Simplicity isn't about what you give up. It's about what you gain. When you remove the things that don't matter, you are free to focus on only the meaningful. Imagine your home and your time filling you with positive energy to help you achieve your dreams. It can happen, and *Organized Simplicity* can show you how.

These books and other fine Betterway Home titles are available at your local bookstore and from online suppliers.
Visit our website at www.betterwaybooks.com.